CW00435370

NAVAL SURFACE WEAPONS

BRASSEY'S SEA POWER: Naval Vessels,
Weapons Systems and Technology Series:
Volume 6

Brassey's Sea Power:
Naval Vessels, Weapons Systems and Technology Series

General Editor: Dr G. Till, Royal Naval College, Greenwich and Department of War Studies, King's College, London

This series, consisting of twelve volumes, aims to explore the impact of modern technology on the size, shape and role of contemporary navies. Using case studies from around the world it explains the principles of naval operations and the functions of naval vessels, aircraft and weapons systems. Each volume is written by an acknowledged expert in a clear, easy-to-understand style and is well illustrated with photographs and diagrams. The series will be invaluable for naval officers under training and also will be of great interest to young professionals and naval enthusiasts.

Volume 1 — Modern Sea Power
  Dr Geoffrey Till

Volume 2 — Ships, Submarines and the Sea
  Dr P. J. Gates and N. M. Lynn

Volume 3 — Surface Ships: An Introduction to Design Principles
  Dr P. J. Gates

Volume 4 — Amphibious Operations: The Projection of Sea Power Ashore
  Colonel M. H. H. Evans

Volume 5 — Naval Electronic Warfare
  Dr D. G. Kiely

Volume 6 — Naval Surface Weapons
  Dr D. G. Kiely

Other series published by Brassey's

Brassey's Land Warfare: New Battlefield Weapons Systems and Technology Series,

12 Volume Set
General Editor: Colonel R. G. Lee, OBE

Brassey's Air Power: Aircraft, Weapons Systems and Technology Series,
  12 Volume Set
General Editor: Air Vice Marshal R. A. Mason, CBE, CB, MA, RAF

For full details of titles in the three series, please contact your local Brassey's/Pergamon Office

Frontispiece: HMS *Illustrious* at sea in 1985. (*Photo: NATO EASTLANT*)

NAVAL
SURFACE WEAPONS

by

DR D. G. KIELY

Foreword by
Admiral of the Fleet Sir John Fieldhouse GCB, GBE

BRASSEY'S DEFENCE
PUBLISHERS
(a member of the Maxwell Pergamon Publishing Corporation plc)

LONDON · OXFORD · WASHINGTON · NEW YORK · BEIJING
FRANKFURT · SÃO PAULO · SYDNEY · TOKYO · TORONTO

U.K. Editorial)	Brassey's Defence Publishers Ltd., 24 Gray's Inn Road, London WC1X 8HR
(Orders)	Brassey's Defence Publishers Ltd., Headington Hill Hall, Oxford OX3 0BW, England
U.S.A. (Editorial)	Pergamon-Brassey's International Defense Publishers, Inc., 8000 Westpark Drive, Fourth Floor, McLean, Virginia 22102, U.S.A.
(Orders)	Pergamon Press, Inc., Maxwell House, Fairview Park, Elmsford, New York 10523, U.S.A.
PEOPLE'S REPUBLIC OF CHINA	Pergamon Press, Room 4037, Qianmen Hotel, Beijing, People's Republic of China
FEDERAL REPUBLIC OF GERMANY	Pergamon Press GmbH, Hammerweg 6, D-6242 Kronberg, Federal Republic of Germany
BRAZIL	Pergamon Editora Ltda, Rua Eça de Queiros, 346, CEP 04011, Paraiso, São Paulo, Brazil
AUSTRALIA	Pergamon-Brassey's Defence Publishers Pty Ltd., P.O. Box 544, Potts Point, N.S.W. 2011, Australia
JAPAN	Pergamon Press, 5th Floor, Matsuoka Central Building, 1-7-1 Nishishinjuku, Shinjuku-ku, Tokyo 160, Japan
CANADA	Pergamon Press Canada Ltd., Suite No. 271, 253 College Street, Toronto, Ontario, Canada, M5T 1R5

First edition 1988

Library of Congress Cataloging in Publication Data
Kiely, D. G. (David G.)
Naval surface weapons/D. G. Kiely; foreword by Sir John Fieldhouse. — 1st ed.
p.   cm. — Brassey's sea power; v. 6)
1. Weapons systems.   I. Title.   II. Series.
VF346.K54 1988   359.8'2 — dc19   88-19819

British Library Cataloguing in Publication Data
Kiely, D. G.
Naval surface weapons.
1. Naval weapon systems
I. Title
623.8'251

ISBN 0-08-036689-9 Hard cover
ISBN 0-08-036688-0 Flexicover

The front cover illustration depicts USS *New Jersey* (United States Navy Naval Forces)

Printed in Great Britain by A. Wheaton & Co. Ltd., Exeter

Acknowledgements

The author acknowledges with thanks the provision of information and illustrations from the following companies:

British Aerospace
Aerospatiale
Contraves
Turner Martin and Partners
BMARC
Hollandse Signaalapparaten
Short Brothers
Oto Melara
Vickers Shipbuilding and Engineering
Breda Meccanica Bresciana
Kongsberg

The author appreciates with thanks the help obtained from constructive discussions with Rear Admiral G. M. K. Brewer CB and wishes to acknowledge with gratitude the assistance of Elisabeth Goulding in the preparation of the manuscript.

The kind assistance of Mr David Foxwell, Editor of *Naval Forces*, who generously provided a number of photographs from his archive, is very much appreciated.

In making this overview, there has been no intention that the comparative reviews of types of equipment should in any way be interpreted as a criticism or commendation of any particular system, component or material.

Contents

List of Figures   ix

Glossary   xi

Foreword by Admiral of the Fleet Sir John Fieldhouse GCB, GBE   xv

1. Introduction   1

2. Operational Employment of Surface Weapons   5
General Assessments—Appreciation of the Situation   5
Threat Assessment   6
Naval Gunfire Support   8
Organic Air Support   8
Air Defence—Defence in Depth   9
Saturation Attacks and Multiple Channels of Fire   11
Pickets   12
Mutual Protection or Self-defence   12
Operational Role of the Medium Calibre Naval Gun   13
Naval Gunfire Support in Amphibious Operations   16

3. The Influence of New Technology   18
Naval Gun Technology   18
Naval Missile Technology   22
Information Technology   26
Naval Weapon System Architecture   26

4. Naval Guns and Guided Projectiles   31
General Purpose Manually Operated Guns   32
Larger Calibre Naval Guns   36
Close-in Weapon Systems   43
Guided Projectiles   54

5. Anti-ship Missiles   57
Penguin   57
Exocet   62
Sea Eagle   67
Sea Skua   70
Otomat   73
A Small Anti-ship Missile for Submarines—SLAM   76

6. Point Defence Missiles   77

   Seawolf   77
   Albatros   80
   Seastreak and Seacat   80

7. Area Defence Missiles   85

   Sea Dart   86
   Lightweight Sea Dart   89
   Support Defence Missile System   92

8. Merchant Ships as Weapon Platforms   93

9. The Way Ahead   98

   General Trends   98
   Guns, Automation and New Weapons   100
   Higher Reliability and Total Weapon Systems   101
   Future Missiles   104

Self-Test Questions   110

About the Author   114

Index   115

List of Figures

Cover: USS *New Jersey*

Frontispiece: HMS *Illustrious* at sea in 1985

FIG. 1.1   Italian Navy hydrofoil craft armed with Otomat missiles and
Oto Melara 76 millimetre gun   4

FIG. 2.1   HMS *Jupiter*, fitted with Seawolf and Exocet missiles   10

FIG. 2.2   A modern fast patrol craft made by Vosper Thorneycroft   11

FIG. 2.3   Israeli Navy Type SAAR 4 warship fitted with Harpoon and
Gabriel II surface-to-surface missiles with Vulcan Phalanx gun
forward and 65 millimetre gun aft   13

FIG. 3.1   Vertical Trials Barge *Longbow*   24

FIG. 3.2   A sequence in the vertical launching of Seawolf   25

FIG. 3.3   Bofors 57 millimetre Mark 2 dual-purpose gun on board the
Swedish coastal corvette *Stockholm*   27

FIG. 3.4   HMS *Illustrious* with Vulcan Phalanx guns fore and aft and
Sea Dart surface-to-air missiles   30

FIG. 4.1   Oerlikon 20 millimetre A41A gun   32

FIG. 4.2   Oerlikon 30 millimetre Anti-Aircraft Gun GCM AO3   34

FIG. 4.3   Oto Melara 35 millimetre twin gun   36

FIG. 4.4   127/54 OTO Compact Gun   39

FIG. 4.5   Vickers 4.5 inch Mark 8 Naval Gun   41

FIG. 4.6   Breda Fast Forty CIWS   45

FIG. 4.7   Breda Fast Forty magazines   46

FIG. 4.8   Goalkeeper CIWS showing radars and guns   49

FIG. 4.9   The Seaguard System   51

FIG. 4.10 Seaguard's guns firing vertically   53

FIG. 4.11 Oto Melara 76 millimetre Super Rapid gun   55

FIG. 5.1   Details of the Penguin Missile   59

ix

FIG. 5.2   Launching Penguin from a small ship   61

FIG. 5.3   Damage to a minelayer by Penguin   62

FIG. 5.4   Exocet firing from a ship   65

FIG. 5.5   The next generation of Exocet—ANS   67

FIG. 5.6   Ship-Launched Sea Eagle   69

FIG. 5.7   Sea Skua in flight   72

FIG. 5.8   Ship-Launched Sea Skua   73

FIG. 5.9   Construction of the Otomat Missile   74

FIG. 5.10 Flight profile of Otomat   75

FIG. 6.1   Seawolf firing from a ship of the Royal Navy   79

FIG. 6.2   Seacat engagement systems   81

FIG. 6.3   Seacat firing from a multiple shipboard launcher   82

FIG. 6.4   General appearance of Seastreak and its three darts   83

FIG. 7.1   Main features of Sea Dart Missile   86

FIG. 7.2   Sea Dart launcher on board HMS *Illustrious*   87

FIG. 7.3   Sea Dart firing   88

FIG. 7.4   Sea Dart operation in relation to missile guidance and target illumination   91

FIG. 7.5   Lightweight Sea Dart target interception range brackets   92

FIG. 8.1   Helicopter support ship RFA *Reliant*. Converted from 23,000 tonne container ship   96

FIG. 9.1   Libyan frigate *DAT Assawari*   102

FIG. 9.2   Royal Netherlands Navy's Guided Weapons Destroyer *Tromp*   103

FIG. 9.3   Modern Norwegian patrol craft firing the Penguin Missile   104

FIG. 9.4   ASTER—general appearance   106

FIG. 9.5   The price of an inadequate anti-missile defence—the hit of an Exocet   107

FIG. 9.6   Swedish Navy's first *Spica II* fast patrol boat at speed   108

Glossary

AA	Anti-Aircraft.
AAW	Anti-air warfare.
AEW	Airborne Early Warning.
AIO	Action Information Organisation—the command centre of a ship.
AOR	Auxiliary Oiler and Replenishment ship.
APDS	Armour Piercing Discarding Sabot.
ASM	Air-to-Surface Missile.
ASS	Aviation Support Ship.
Base bleed	A pyrotechnic attachment to the end of a shell which reduces drag during flight.
BLPG	Bulk loaded liquid propellant gun.
Cardinal Points Procurement	A method of procurement involving competition, a specification of desirable performance characteristics, and a dialogue with the supply industry to assist alignment with exports.
CIC	Combat Information Centre—another term for the AIO.
CIWS	Close In Weapon System—for very short range air defence out to a few kilometres.
Clutter	Unwanted radar echoes from land, sea, rain, snow or other sources.
CSM	Common Support Module.
CW	Continuous wave.
DF	Direction finding.
ECCM	Electronic counter countermeasures.
ELINT	Electronic Intelligence.
EMCON	Emission control—radio silence.
ESM	Electronic Support Measures—passive electronic warfare.
EW	Electronic Warfare.
FLIR	Forward Looking Infra-Red
Frequency Bands C, I, K, Ku, X	Parts of the microwave spectrum.
Glint	Movement of the point of radar lock on a complex target due to interference between reflections from different parts of it.
Graceful degradation	A gradual or part failure, as opposed to total failure, of a weapon system to leave a residual capability.
Hardware	Equipment (as opposed to software).
HEI	High explosive incendiary ammunition.

Hz	Hertz, cycles per second. A measure of the periodicity of a wave and used as a measure of the stiffness of a structure in relation to its mechanical resonance.
IR	Infra-red.
KN	Kilonewton. A measure of force. One newton imparts an acceleration of 1 metre per second per second to 1 kilogram.
MLRS	Multiple Launch Rocket System.
Modular construction	A means of constructing systems from a limited number of equipment modules which may be used in different combinations to yield different systems.
MRBS	Mean Rounds Between Stoppages.
MTI	Moving Target Indication.
MV	Muzzle Velocity.
Naval Application Officers	Naval officers used in weapon development teams as expert users or maintainers to assist project managers.
NGS	Naval Gunfire Support.
Organic air support	Support given to ships by aircraft borne in ships.
Penetrators	Sharp darts made from very hard metal employed to pierce missiles and explode their warheads.
PDMS	Point Defence Missile System.
PGM	Precision Guided Munition—guided shells.
Point defence	Self defence.
PPI	Plan position indicator of a radar.
Ripple fire	A stream of closely spaced missiles from one or a number of directions to saturate the defence systems.
RLPG	Regenerative liquid propellant gun.
Sabot	A case fitting around the base of a projectile to make it fit the rifling of a barrel. Used with penetrators.
SACLOS	Semi-automatic command to line-of-sight.
SCADS	Seaborne Containerised Air Defence System.
Sea Skimmer	A missile which uses an altimeter to fly low over the sea and thus under the beams of conventional air defence radars.
Smart projectile	One with a capability of guiding itself to its target.
Software	The programme, instructions and stored data used by a processer or computer.
STUFT	Ships taken up from trade.
SWSA	Ship Weapon System Authority.
System Architecture	The overall design of an assembly of equipment and programmes (hardware and software) to carry out, collectively a function.
TEWA	Threat evaluation and weapon allocation.
TIR	Tracking and illuminating radar.
TP	Training ammunition.
TWS	Track while scan.
TWT	Travelling wave tube.
Vertical bunt	In the final stage of a missile's trajectory a sharp rise followed by sharp fall to the target.

VLS	Vertically launched missile system.
VLSI	Very large scale integration—integrated circuits with very many components on a semi-conductor chip.
VTOL	Vertical take off and landing aircraft.
Zenith capability	The capability to fire vertically upwards.

Foreword

By Admiral of the Fleet Sir John Fieldhouse GCB, GBE
Chief of the Defence Staff

For over five centuries the naval gun dominated maritime warfare and largely dictated the design of the ships that carried it as their main armament. More recently, the advent of the submarine, mine, aircraft and missile have all presented challenges to the supremacy of the surface vessel as the instrument of naval policy and all now have their place, with interwoven roles, in the maritime tapestry. The result, in the surface ship, has been a complex range of offensive and defensive weapons that, in various combinations, often linked to a central command system, provides modern warships with their above water warfighting capability.

It is a matter of fact that the Royal Navy has been in the van in this process of evolution, the pace of which has never been faster than it is today. In the equipment field, the last twenty years have seen the transition of the digital computer from the esoteric to the commonplace, so that it is now an essential prerequisite in present day weapon systems. The speed and intricacy of the battle has made increasing demands upon the officers required to conduct it and, in the development field, it is important that this first-hand experience is brought into play in concert with the work of the scientist and engineer. The author is careful to make this point and also quotes the example of the Falklands conflict and its impact on the maritime scene.

Dr Kiely writes with authority and his knowledge and personal experience in the Service research and development field are evident. The result is a highly readable volume which could be regarded as an unofficial reference book on Naval Surface Weapons; it is certainly well suited to a wide readership.

1

Introduction

Naval surface weapons, together with underwater weapons, are the prime *raison d'être* of surface warships. While these ships can, and do, fulfil useful naval purposes by their very presence in certain circumstances, by showing the flag and by acting in diplomatic and ceremonial roles, their essential task and their marine significance is as weapon carriers. The weapons are now generally assembled into total systems together with their associated sensors. The systems, designed as complete entities, have the three main purposes of offence, self-defence of the ship and the defence of ships in company. Naval surface weapon systems are now very complex and increasingly use software and data processors in their control and operation. Their design is difficult and sophisticated since the total systems must work reliably and with the minimum mutual interference in the close confines of a moving metal hull which, unlike an aircraft or tank, spends long periods away from its base and maintenance facility. This is one major factor which has always governed the design of ship weapon systems.

For modern installations, we can identify three further important factors which have had a major influence on naval weapons. First, the speed of naval engagements is increasing, due to the presence now of very fast, long-range missiles and aircraft. Attacks can develop very quickly and there is very little time for men to appreciate the situation, make decisions and give orders to initiate defensive responses. This leads to the need for totally automatic responses from software-controlled weapons where the threat assessment and the decision to open fire, or take some other action, is done by data processors.

The second important factor is the advent of the sea-skimming missile which is undoubtedly the most potent and significant naval threat in modern times because it is extremely difficult to detect until it is virtually at its target. This again causes the time of the engagement, when defences can be brought to bear, to be extremely short and typically less than 30 seconds. This factor has had a truly profound effect upon naval tactics and weapons and is really the most fundamental change in modern naval engagements, since it alters the balance of man–machine control very significantly towards the machine. The reason why the sea-skimming missile is difficult to detect by the victim ship's radar is not an equipment failing but is quite fundamental. An object close to the boundary between the air and the sea is difficult to illuminate by a ship's radar. The boundary is a reflector and the normal type of radar beam is effectively bent upwards by the process of interaction between direct and reflected radar rays.

The third important factor is the great and significant contribution made by modern technology, both hardware and software, to the capability of modern weapon systems in terms of reaction time, fire power and general versatility. In consequence, present-day naval weapons with vertically launched missiles, very fast firing guns, automatic target selection, automatic system operation and long range and accuracy have a formidable performance which gives to surface ships a potent capability for attack and defence.

With increasing technical sophistication there is an inevitable concern, and a problem, about reliability. The skill in system design is to maintain an acceptable balance between high performance and adequate availability. Thus, in the weapon systems of today, a new requirement has grown in the need for system architecture to be carried out in a formal, orderly and quantitative manner to produce optimum sets of equipments which will work together to give best cost-effectiveness in performance and reliability. The advent of the weapon system concept is a new and important feature of naval surface weapons which now cannot be ignored. It is bound to beome more significant.

An important and very necessary element in naval weapon systems design and development is a close and effective partnership between the civilian engineer and the naval user. This is required to ensure that the right choice of technology is made to yield weapons with adequate performance to meet threats and with operational and environmental characteristics which suit shipboard conditions. With so much technological capability available, and limited financial resources, the basic problem is one of choice rather than one of invention. The choice must embrace cost, performance, reliability and operating characteristics to suit shipboard conditions.

In the United Kingdom, the use of the Naval Application Officer principle makes this process of choice much easier. Application Officers are expert users and maintainers and they are appointed to weapon project teams to contribute in these rôles, not as designers. In Government Establishments, serving naval officers are used for application duties and in industry, where most of the design is carried out, advice is also given by retired officers. The result is that British weapon systems are likely to be particularly cost-effective and also well matched to shipboard conditions. The Application Officer principle grew up from experience in World War II, but it is even more relevant today when technology can achieve virtually any performance at a price. This effective partnership between user and supplier, which is so well established as a normal procedure in British weapon system design, is an important contributory factor in the success of weapon systems in Royal Navy ships.

In a technology-rich climate, such as we have today, the actual method of procuring weapons from industry is also important to their cost-effectiveness and reliability. If the naval user is given freedom to specify in detailed engineering terms precisely what he would choose to have, the result is likely to be over-complex, over-costly and unreliable, though quite practicable from current technology. A much more cost-effective outcome is achieved by the British method of Cardinal Points procurement in which the Ministry of Defence states only the 'cardinal points' of the performance and characteristics it would like to see in the weapon and invites fixed price competition for production equipments from industry to meet as many as possible of these cardinal points. The element of competition ensures realistic prices and the judgement of industry is allowed to assess how much complexity and sophistication to include within the fixed price offered. This leads to a minimum of technological risk and so to better inherent reliability, while going as far as is considered prudent, both financially and technically, to meet all the cardinal points. Thus more realistic and more reliable equipment, with adequate performance, is likely to be a feature of naval surface weapon systems from British industry which must compete in the world market as well as serve the Royal Navy.

The good 'pedigree' of British naval weapons is based on the evolution of a process of relationship between the Navy, the supply industry and the Procurement Executive of the Ministry of Defence in which each of the three participants is able to contribute its own influence in emergent weapons in an appropriately balanced proportion. The result is a blend of adequate performance to meet current threats from the use of advanced, but not unproven, technology, to yield reliability and good cost-effectiveness for the entire world market. The relationship between these three participants is perhaps often overlooked, but it is both subtle and sophisticated. It is undoubtedly influential in the creation of good quality naval weapons.

The quality of technology and design in the naval surface weapons now being offered on the world market by companies from other European countries and the United States is unquestionably very high. Navies today are fortunate in having such a rich choice of excellent weapon systems available to them, by whatever processes they are created. Competition between comparable weapons on the world market is strong and healthy and is helping to increase cost-effectiveness. In most cases, it forms the basis of the procurement policies of navies. While British weapons are excellent, the forces of competition have resulted in some other guns and missiles being included in the weapon systems of the Royal Navy, and a similar type of international mix is not uncommon in many other navies.

Whatever their purpose in naval tactics, modern surface weapon systems are likely to be influenced in their design by all the factors discussed above. The outcome is that the navies of today may acquire the most impressive capabilities in their surface ships, which contribute markedly to the continuing importance of sea power in international affairs. No longer is a large surface ship necessary to achieve a major naval weapon capability. Modern weapons can confer a very significant naval capability on quite small hulls, as is discussed in the following chapters. Today, naval power can be more widely distributed internationally and can enable small ship navies to be much more effective than ever they were before.

An excellent example is the small hydrofoil craft of the Italian Navy which is shown in Figure 1.1. This little vessel has two Otomat sea-skimming anti-ship missiles and a 76-mm gun with a rate of fire of 120 rounds per minute. This fire power is enough to sink a frigate and shoot down several aircraft and is available in a hull of size comparable to that of a helicopter. However, it must be appreciated that it is sometimes difficult to find space in small hulls for all the command and control and targeting facilities to enable full use to be made of long-range weapons; an attendant aircraft or helicopter may be necessary to give assistance in weapon control.

The weapon system is now more important than the size of hull in governing sea power. In modern frigates the weapon system cost accounts for approximately half the total ship cost, while some 30 or 40 years ago it was typically no more than 10–20 percent of the total. This is, perhaps, no more than appropriate when, in reality, the ship is primarily a weapon carrier and the major part of its cost should be accounted for by the weapon system.

In the chapters which follow, the impact of these influences on modern weapon

Fig. 1.1   Italian Navy hydrofoil craft armed with Otomat missiles and Oto Melara 76 millimetre gun. (*Photo: Oto Melara*)

systems in ships will be discussed, together with the operational attitudes towards their tactical employment. The intention in this book is to provide an overview, in perspective, of the main features of modern naval surface weapons, of the technical aspects of their design and performance and the philosophy of their employment within the fabric of naval tactics and the scenarios of the strategic deployment of warships. The subject is extensive and complex, but the principal features and the highlights will serve to give a realistic impression of the way in which surface weapon systems have evolved in present-day ships, meeting current threats by means of the application of the rich technology which is now available to weapon designers.

2

Operational Employment of Surface Weapons

GENERAL ASSESSMENTS—APPRECIATION OF THE SITUATION

In naval surface engagements it would seem that there has long been a sense of realism in self-preservation and the avoidance of unnecessary threats. This is made clear by Captain John Smith, writing his book *The Sea-Man's Grammar* in London in 1653, where he says:

> *How to manage a fight at sea, 1653.*
> *The Captain gives the command: "Make fast your grapplings," whereupon one reports to him: "Captain, we are fowl on each other, and the Ship is on fire." Cut anything to get clear, and smother the fire with wet clothes. In such a case they will presently be such friends as to help one the other all they can to get clear, lest they both should burn together and sink, and if they be generous, the fire quenched, drink kindely one to another; heave their cans over boord, and then begin again as before.*

Nowadays, while the situation is more complex, perhaps the same sentiments of sound common sense and priorities remain!

As a general background to the employment of surface weapons, it may be helpful to review the type of operational considerations which arise when a naval task is being planned by a commander and his staff. While only a very general and typical overview is appropriate here it may, perhaps, assist in giving some conception of how weapon capabilities are interwoven with tactical and other naval considerations in planning an operation and hence provide a realistic perspective of the part played by weapons and sensors in the overall fabric of naval affairs at sea.

The aim of the operation should ideally be formulated so that it is simple and undivided, but this is often difficult as conflicting factors can occur. For example, the aim of the 'safe and timely' arrival of a convoy may involve a conflict between 'safe' and 'timely'. It might well be more practicable to achieve greater safety by a course of action which takes more time; should the cargoes of damaged ships be saved by slowing down the entire convoy to stay with the victims, or should they be left behind or sunk to allow the rest to proceed rapidly? Such decisions must be reviewed by the commander when formulating his aim.

The nature of the operation, offensive or defensive, must be considered and here it may be necessary to lay what may seem to be undue emphasis on defensive measures by the ships, even if their task in the operation is offensive, such as providing naval gunfire support ashore for a land battle. But this is entirely appropriate as it is essential to preserve the ships from possible air or underwater threats whilst the prime offensive or defensive task is being carried out. Hence, friendly forces available for the task must be examined together with their collective capabilities for offence and defence which will include their ability to give mutual support to one another. Space and time factors must be reviewed, together with any problems of navigation; can the ships go quickly and directly to the area concerned? May they divert for reasons of safety or tactical advantage? Or are they confined to a specific course for reasons of geography or time? The weather, both in terms of known patterns and actual forecasts, is a vital factor which can affect sensor and weapon performance as well as navigation. Visibility, radar sea clutter, wave height affecting the altitude of sea skimmers, as well as a threat of collision and grounding in fog during periods of radar silence, are all consequences of the weather and its effect on equipment performance.

The depth of the water and the nature of the sea bottom will have a bearing on the practicability of a mine threat, as well as on submarine operations and a torpedo threat. Operations close to land, as in the Falklands War, can have a major effect on the performance of sensors and weapons in that the land may provide cover for an approaching air strike so that it might be undetected by the ship's sensors until the last few seconds. Weapon performance may thus be impaired, and the weapon sensors may need a doppler or MTI (moving target indication) capability to see targets against a background of land clutter. Conversely, the ships may be able to gain an advantage of concealment from nearby land masses against enemy sensors. All of these, and other, general factors affecting the operation must be considered in relation to their effect upon the ship's weapons and sensors. When the appropriate conclusions are reached, plans must be drawn up to take them into account from the very start of preparation for the operation.

THREAT ASSESSMENT

This done, the threat which might be expected from the enemy must be assessed as well as any possible self-imposed threats of collision or grounding, due perhaps to restrictions on the use of radio navigation exacerbated by bad weather.

The weapon threat posed by the enemy is, of course, assessed with much dependence on intelligence information. Essentially, that assessment must include what surveillance capability is available to the enemy from aircraft, satellites or underwater devices, whether or not these give a real time capability and what geographic areas they can cover in relation to radii of action from enemy bases. It will also include any DF and ESM capability he is known to have, any air or seaborne shadowing capability and any relocation possibilities. From all this a short list of a refined surveillance threat can be drawn up.

The enemy's weapon capability is assessed in terms of what weapons could be brought within range, again in relation to radii of action from enemy bases, the attack patterns involved, including the stand-off launching of missiles, visual aiming of non-guided projectiles, 'smart' devices, such as precision guided munitions, and sea-skimmers. Again, a realistic refined threat is assessed for the operation concerned which, for geographic or other reasons may eliminate certain possible threats.

At this stage, the commander of the operation will use his judgement to decide what he is most likely to be up against and draw up his dispositions and formations accordingly. The underwater threat may affect ship spacing to give an effective sonar screen, and the air threat may involve the stationing of forward air defence picket ships to give early warning. An organic AEW (airborne early warning) radar in a shipborne helicopter is likely to be a very valuable source of early warning and, in particular, of warning of low-flying aircraft and missiles.

Very broadly, the commander will wish to deny the enemy the opportunity of getting into a firing position with his weapon and, indeed, also of obtaining identification, range and bearing of the ships in the operation. He will be concerned with creating a disposition and formation of his ships and aircraft to achieve this if he can and to provide such mutual support as is practicable. Many factors of command and control, as well as weapon and sensor performance, are involved in this complex and very important assessment.

Next, the commander and his staff must consider what is the best way to counter the threat using their own weapons and sensors, and also the best way to carry out the offensive part of the operation if one is involved. They will probably consider if the operation can be carried out without engaging the enemy, or if not what would be an acceptable exchange rate of loss. In an extreme case, it could be acceptable to have a loss rate of 100 percent to achieve a vitally important objective.

In general, the commander will first examine how to defeat the enemy sensors by keeping the vehicles far enough away, by using EMCON (emission control) to give no help to enemy ESM (electronic support measures—listening devices), to blind or confuse a satellite or airborne radar by electronic warfare, or by using concealment from land masses. Warships can be remarkably difficult to find and identify in the open ocean if they do not give themselves away by radiating characteristic signals from radars or communications equipment, or by using distinctive formations. A search can be a very slow business, involving many ships over an extensive area of sea and calling for the use of radar, ELINT and photographic reconnaissance by satellite or aircraft.

Having decided this, the commander must then consider how best to deploy his own weapons against the assessed refined threat in order to reduce its lethality. He will have to consider the advantages and disadvantages of EMCON, the ability of his weapons to counter those of the enemy, the use of decoys and the possible use of confusion using his own EW resources. All this will have a bearing on his overall plan of action and on how he disposes his own ships and aircraft. It is a difficult, complex and vital assessment and one that relies heavily upon the experience and judgement of the commander and his staff. Through it all lies the knowledge of weapon performance which, in this way, is knitted into the detailed planning of naval operations from their beginnings. There is no set pattern to the operational employment of naval surface weapons, only a number of general principles. Each operation, and each commander, gives rise to differences in the way weapons are used. While these are differences in detail within the limits of the weapon capabilities, it is often they which contribute to the use of successful tactics and so to striking operational success. The overall man-machine effectiveness in naval surface weapons is at present as much, or more, governed by the skill of the man as by the performance of the weapon system. This leads us back to the rôle of the Application Officer in weapon system development, for it is largely he who ensures that the weapons' detailed characteristics are such that they can be exploited flexibly, ingeniously and effectively by able commanders at sea. In very fast reaction situations, such as with Close In Weapon Systems (CIWS) and point defence missiles, the weapon control and initiation is necessarily by software because there is no time for men to take decisions, although they can inhibit the weapon. Nevertheless, outside the circumstances of automatic weapon operation, there remains the fundamental requirement for commanders at sea to plan, influence and control the deployment of weapon systems in naval operations.

NAVAL GUNFIRE SUPPORT

Naval gunfire support for land operations uses medium calibre guns, typically of 4.5–6 inch calibre, which, together with their integrated fire control systems, have been developed into extremely accurate weapons capable of delivering shells to designated points at ranges of over 20 kilometres. The fire control system takes account of the tide, wind, ship movement and the ballistic factors so that, as the ship moves, the gun training and elevation is constantly and automatically adjusted to relate to the target ashore. If the target is visible from the ship, the fall of shot can be observed and the gun setting corrected after the first few ranging shots to bring the shells precisely to the target. If the target is not visible from the ship, a forward observer in an aircraft or on the ground is employed to report the fall of shot by radio so that final corrections can be made to the fire control system—effectively, a fine correction or guidance by visual observation. This method of shore bombardment is extremely accurate and effective.

In future, if the gun fires precision guided munitions (PGM) the forward observer may be used to illuminate the target with a laser or microwave illuminator; the reflection from the target would be detected by the shell which would then correct its course to hit it. This is really a technical refinement of the visual reporting method, providing greater accuracy and making gunfire support even more effective. Gunfire with PGM against air targets would also employ an illuminator of some kind, but this could be a radar which monitored the target movement and caused commands to be sent to the shells in flight to correct their course. Whether the shells are purely ballistic or guided surface and air targets are continuously monitored in range, bearing and elevation by a fire control radar. This information is fed into the fire control system which keeps the gun aligned for the target.

Naval gunfire has now been developed into a highly accurate capability. Aided by the advent of PGM, it is currently rising in favour, having been overshadowed by missiles for some decades. A significant consideration is that the cost per shell is much less than that of even the simplest missile.

ORGANIC AIR SUPPORT

The operational concept of using shipborne helicopters to carry sensors aloft is very important and effective. Airborne radar and ESM can be deployed rapidly to provide early warning and warning of low-flying missiles and aircraft which would not be visible to shipborne sensors. Although the endurance of the helicopter may be limited, the ability of a commander to mount an airborne surveillance operation in times of tension is greatly valued. To a degree, it can serve the role of a forward air defence picket ship for a short time. Organic airborne surveillance of this type is particularly important and effective if the radar has a doppler or MTI capability to identify moving targets close to the sea.

AIR DEFENCE – DEFENCE IN DEPTH

For air defence there is a general concept of operations which is accepted by all the larger, ocean-going navies. Indeed, parts of the same concept are used in smaller engagements of a coastal nature. This is the concept of defence in depth, or layered defence, in which a number of different forms of defence are used at different ranges to provide a series of obstacles to reduce the lethality of threats as they attempt to penetrate inwards to the naval force from long range. In this way, the threat is successfully diluted by different weapons operating at different ranges which are best suited to their individual characteristics. The attacker is thereby compelled to prepare himself to counter a number of different forms of defensive measures, which adds very materially to his problem and to his costs.

The outer layer of air defence is usually provided by fighter aircraft carried by the naval force when these are available. This 'organic' air power usually operates at a range of several hundred miles out and its prime task is to attack the enemy weapon carrier before it can launch its weapons against the ships. Weapon carriers would typically be aircraft with anti-ship missiles or bombs, or surface ships with anti-ship missiles. The target information for this outer layer of air defence would come from airborne early warning (AEW) or satellite sensors. It is clearly extremely important to destroy or disable the enemy's weapon carriers before they can launch their attack, particularly if their weapons could constitute or contribute to a saturation attack with a large number of weapons fired simultaneously or near-simultaneously.

The next layer of defence is the medium range missile, such as Sea Dart or Standard Missile, which would operate out to about 100 miles or slightly shorter and would take out those aircraft or missiles which 'leak' through the outer layer. If there is no organic air power in the naval force, then this second layer would become the first or outermost opposition which would confront the attacker. Target information for this layer would most probably come from the ship's own radars, although these might be alerted by AEW.

The next layer of defence would be the ship's medium calibre guns. These could fire precision guided munitions (PGM) to increase their accuracy out to ranges of about 10–15 miles. They would be more effective against aircraft than missiles and have a very positive air defence capability, controlled entirely by shipborne sensors and fire control equipments.

The next layer of defence is provided by the point defence missile systems (PDMS) such as Seawolf. These operate out to a range of about 5–10 kilometres and are completely automatic in operation, because the threats they engage are at quite short ranges and there is no time for a human reaction to decide whether or not to engage. The PDMS have their own sensors and operate as self-contained weapons, controlled by software that is designed to assess the threat and, if appropriate, fire the missiles. The role of the man in this man–machine relationship is to inhibit or abort the

FIG. 2.1   A Royal Navy Leander class frigate, HMS *Jupiter*, fitted with Seawolf and Exocet
missiles. (*Photo: Ferranti Computer Systems Ltd/Naval Forces*)

automatic weapon if he has good reason to do so; he does not initiate the firing which
is done by the software. Of course the really essential role of the man is played
beforehand in the writing of the software and ensuring that it will be both safe and
effective in its powers of discrimination between false and friendly targets.

The final layer of the air defence is the close-in weapon system (CIWS). This
operates out to about 3 kilometres but usually concentrates on the final 1.5
kilometres. This is the 'last ditch' defence and is provided by fast firing guns such as
Seaguard or Goalkeeper and the hybrid missile—PGM systems, such as Seastreak.
These are completely automatic systems with their own sensors and they can provide
a devastating degree of fire power at short range. Electronic warfare decoys are also
used in this final layer of defence.

With all these layers, a force can have a very effective measure of air defence
available to it, but it must be acknowledged that in some, or many situations not all
the layers will be provided in naval task forces, groups of ships or single ships. Most
ships will carry CIWS and possibly also PDMS, while the outer layers will be shared
and provided by specialist ships for the protection of a group. The principle of a
layered defence in depth is, without question, extremely sound and very effective in
practice.

A layered air defence gives the attacker a multiple problem in having to make his

FIG. 2.2   A modern fast patrol craft made by Vosper Thorneycroft.
(*Photo: Vosper Thorneycroft/Naval Forces*)

weapon capable of functioning through a number of different types of assault on it. This, as already indicated above, leads to complexity and cost penalties to meet so very flexible and varied an array of defence measures. But layered air defence also gives the defender himself a problem over the command and control of such an array of defensive measures, particularly over the co-ordination and the allocation of targets to weapons in order to avoid duplication of engagements and so to gain the maximum effectiveness from the whole. Suffice it to say that this is a complex problem which is addressed in the software of the action information organisation (AIO) where one of the central tasks is known as TEWA (standing for Threat Evaluation and Weapon Allocation). Since the software to be employed in AIOs must be real time in nature, these command systems inevitably involve much difficulty and complexity in the devising of extremely large programmes to meet a very wide range of operational scenarios. They represent, in fact, probably the most complex and advanced application of real time software in any application of data processing. They are still evolving in order to meet the demands of naval operations.

SATURATION ATTACKS AND MULTIPLE CHANNELS OF FIRE

To overcome the defence in depth concept, the trend in air attacks on ships is towards saturation of the defence by presenting a number of targets in the air simultaneously, or near-simultaneously. This complicates the problems of the defence very considerably in that it provides a lot more target data to be assessed in order to select the most serious threats and deal with them in priority. Furthermore, it creates the need for more channels of fire in order to engage several missiles or aircraft at once, rather than sequentially. If the multiple attacks come from different directions simultaneously, the problem for the defence is even worse as the defending weapons must be able to change their points of aim very rapidly.

To meet this most demanding circumstance, the number of CIWS installations in the larger ships may be increased, but the most significant response from modern technology has been to create the vertically launched missile for PDMS. With vertical launching, a number of missiles may be sent up at once and then directed towards different targets on to which they home independently. In this way, a much greater number of channels of fire are created and the problem of the obstruction of a conventional launcher by the the ship's superstructure is also overcome. Thus, the pattern of air attack and defence is now set for the future as one of saturation attacks and multiple channels of fire for defence, and this trend is most likely to continue.

PICKETS

If there is no organic air element with the naval force, its commander may decide to station one ship well ahead of the main body to act as an air defence picket and give early warning of an approaching attack from its radar or ESM. While this could give a very valuable degree of early warning, the solitary picket is vulnerable without the support of the rest of the force. It must be capable of defending itself adequately in order to minimise the risk created by exposing it in this way, as experience showed in the Falklands War.

MUTUAL PROTECTION OR SELF-DEFENCE

One of the current questions being addressed in many naval circles is both operational and technical, and relates to whether it is better to protect a ship in company, typically a merchant ship or a Fleet Auxiliary, by installing on it a gun or missile system in containers or to provide a warship to give it close support with a PDMS of extended range. This method of mutual air defence would be considerably more costly than a conventional PDMS, but it could be deployed in the warship to serve different merchant ships with, perhaps more flexibility and less expense than providing a large number of containerised weapon systems for the merchant ships. However, in these circumstances, the warship would be totally committed to its merchant ship charges and could not be used for much, if anything, else. Thus, in such a situation, the cost of the air defence would be the total cost of the warship while it was so engaged. No solution to this problem of choice will be put forward here but the issue is raised to illustrate the type of question now being addressed in the operational employment of naval surface weapons. It is a problem of cost, and to some extent of operational flexibility. Technically, extended range PDMS, or as they are now termed, support defence missile systems (SDMS) can be made and are currently being studied. Equally, containerised weapon systems are perfectly practicable and do exist in various forms. The choice rests on how the costs are assessed in through life terms and it is not unlikely that in future both forms of defence will be found in operational service in different scenarios and under different circumstances.

OPERATIONAL ROLE OF THE MEDIUM CALIBRE NAVAL GUN

Naval gunnery is currently enjoying a return to favour in operational circles and it is appropriate to review the role of the medium calibre gun as it is seen, typically, by a leading manufacturer, Vickers Shipbuilding and Engineering Limited which makes the 4.5 inch MK 8 naval gun.

The Falklands campaign proved the need for the Royal Navy to deploy a fleet based on a balanced mix of weapons, particularly if it is to assume several rôles whilst operating in a high threat environment. Since then the Royal Navy, as has the United States Navy, following its action in the Lebanon and the Persian Gulf, recognised the importance of the medium calibre gun in contemporary operations. However, there are few, if any, medium calibre guns in use which can truly claim to be representative of the new technology now available. That both the Royal Navy and the United States Navy should have reverted to arming ships with a mix of medium calibre guns and missile systems, instead of developing all-missile armed ships, is probably the best evidence that the medium calibre gun still has an important rôle to play. Most

Fig. 2.3   An Israeli Navy Type SAAR 4 warship fitted with Harpoon and Gabriel II surface-to-surface missiles. The Vulcan Phalanx gun is forward with a 65 millimetre gun aft.
(*Photo: Naval Forces*)

navies stipulate that new procurements of surface warships must, if not fitted with a medium calibre gun, be fitted for one. Unfortunately, whilst the design and construction of the warship as a platform has generally kept pace with modern technology, the same cannot be said of the medium calibre gun, the majority of which were designed twenty or more years ago. Between entering service and now, the only advances, through product improvement programmes, have been confined to increasing the firing rate whilst reducing the weight and size of mountings.

The all-missile ship was set to become the 'jewel' in the naval crown, largely leaving the protagonists of the naval gun with the remnants of the available technology and finances. This philosophy stemmed from the widespread introduction of the anti-ship missile into most navies, the increasing importance of AAW, and the relatively poor capability of gunfire prediction systems to handle manoeuvring targets when compared with the ability of missiles to counter the ASM threat. The Falklands, albeit not a typical campaign, demonstrated the need to win sea control and to exercise it if a navy is satisfactorily to undertake a power projection role. One factor that did emerge from this campaign was that, apart from the sinking of the General Belgrano, there were few actions between warships since the submarine presence tended to restrict surface warship movements. Land-based air forces were used to attempt to destroy the British task force, which was trying to exercise sea power without gaining air superiority. However, once the Argentinian air threat had been contained to a great extent, the task force then closed on the disputed islands to provide shore bombardment by naval guns and to land troops in amphibious operations.

Until this time, sea power and the supporting technology had been very much tilted towards the ship and missile systems, either making them more effective or dedicated to destroying them. Yet highly developed and specialised vessels and missile systems cannot project power by transporting a task force, nor can they 'police' a blockade in anything but the highest intensity warfare. In effect, during the Falklands campaign, the Royal Navy proved the need to deploy a fleet based on a balanced mix of weapons systems, particularly when operating in a high threat environment necessitating the undertaking of several rôles.

In this conflict, as in the Lebanon, the medium calibre gun played an important role in providing naval gunfire in support of amphibious operations. The White Paper on the Falklands Campaign recorded that 'Task force ships fired 8000 rounds of ammunition in accurate Naval gunfire attacks on ground targets' in addition to noting that 4.5-inch guns proved effective and accurate in the anti-surface ship role. Amphibious operations are still a major rôle for navies, the securing or regaining of objectives under hostile attack demanding the response that only these operations can give. It follows that if these operations are to succeed, naval gunfire support for troops ashore will be a major requirement, in addition to giving support in the air defence role.

The requirements for the medium calibre naval gun can therefore be assessed in relation to the traditional rôle of a navy, to win sea control and, once won, to exercise sea power by bringing support to its allies whilst denying support for its enemies. Within these rôles, three specific functions can be identified, naval gunfire support, surface engagement of enemy warships, and air defence. However, as in any project, trying to satisfy a number of requirements with a single solution will present limitations by having to reach a compromise in some areas or characteristics.

The air defence rôle is probably the least important since current thinking indicates that warships will usually have a medium calibre gun only as a back-up to surface-to-air, with CIWS being relied on for close range self-defence. The sinking of HMS *Sheffield* by an air-launched Exocet highlighted the guided anti-ship missile threat, and emphasised a possible vulnerability in surface warships in the age of missile warfare. The defence priority to this threat is to find the aircraft and destroy it before it can fire. The next priority is to destroy the launched weapon or baffle it by electronic countermeasures. Yet with agile anti-ship missiles being in the main, 'fire and forget', changing altitude in mid flight, either descending to hide in wavetop radar clutter or climbing and diving rapidly in the flight terminal phase using programmed evasive manoeuvres, a huge technological effort in fleet defensive weapons systems is needed to counter this threat and the medium calibre gun would not be primarily involved.

The layered defence philosophy is designed to intercept the attacking aircraft in an outer zone, using AEW aircraft, fighter interceptors and electronic warfare aircraft before the ship is within range of the anti-ship missiles the aircraft are carrying. Because of the huge areas of ocean that the outer defence zone must cover, it is difficult fully to monitor it. Thus many anti-ship missiles will probably get through to be engaged by long range area defence missiles. Those enemy anti-ship missiles that get through the outer zone defences and area defences will be attacked by short-range point defences, comprising short-range ship-to-air interceptor missiles, anti-aircraft guns, decoys and electronic warfare systems.

The critical problems are detection, multiple target capability, reaction time, fire power, area coverage, reliability and resistance to countermeasures. The United States Navy's *Aegis* programme aims to provide a leakproof umbrella for its fleets and is based on extended range missiles which appear to form the best solution to the air threat. In the future, the *Aegis* ships will have vertical launch (VLS) missile system using modules which offer more efficient use of shipboard space and all-weather capability. The missile will engage targets at 50 kilometres while, at the other end of the air defence envelope are the superfast reacting CIWS. The problems associated with conventional medium calibre guns regarding prediction and time of flight with purely ballistic shells will effectively preclude such weapons from playing an effective part in the air defence role, at least in the foreseeable future.

Recent conflicts have shown that surface warships have a vital role. However, the very presence of a surface warship, itself a tempting target, makes an enticing option. To this end, several surface engagement weapons exist, a major threat being the intelligent surface-launched anti-ship missile. Survivability therefore depends very largely on defensive weapons, both passive and active, together with composite fleet operations involving special purpose vessels providing the requisite depth of defence.

Returning to the Falklands campaign: the Argentinians, in addition to destroying *Sheffield*, launched an Exocet from a temporary launching platform and damaged the *Glamorgan*, thus demonstrating the missile's advantages over medium calibre guns in range, flexibility and striking power. However, as the missile system is severely limited by magazine capacity the enemy may rapidly exhaust his supply, especially if electronic countermeasures are successful. The gun may therefore prove to be a more effective means overall, both in cost and destructive terms, of delivering fire power than missiles, particularly against less powerful and less important targets. There is, however, a prediction problem for times of flight of 60–70 seconds at ranges of 25–30 kilometres. Precision guided munitions could well be used for this purpose. The medium-calibre gun's rôle is to destroy the target vessel before it has a chance to reach its missile launch position. To say the least, this is not a very hopeful proposition, having due regard to the range from which the missile can be fired and its speed, which reduces the target's allowable reaction time.

Developments in extended range ammunition, using base-bleed technology and rocket assisted projectiles, will somwhat redress the imbalance enabling ships to be engaged at longer ranges. The prime rôle of the gun in a layered defence system will probably be to destroy the enemy vessel's radar sensors using fragmentation warheads with proximity fuzes. Alternatively, special shells, with post impact delay fuzes, can be used to penetrate the vessel's hull, exploding within it to destroy systems and machinery. Other special purpose shells, including decoys and electronic countermeasure devices, can also play a major role for the medium calibre gun in surface engagements.

NAVAL GUNFIRE SUPPORT IN AMPHIBIOUS OPERATIONS

The requirement rapidly to shift targets in support of troops during amphibious operations can only be met by the flexibility and responsiveness of a gun. Whilst the shell requires an adequate explosive capability to destroy targets, the ability to maintain a sustained bombardment of enemy positions is equally important. Besides being a morale booster for friendly forces, it is also a morale destroyer for the enemy and ensures that they remain under cover.

Once the friendly forces have landed and the forward edges of the battle area close, the chief requirement in addition to sustaining fire, is for accuracy. Current conventional shell technology enables repeatable high accuracy to be maintained giving the user navy the added benefit that expensive and sophisticated sensors, as needed in the AA role, are not required. Throughout the operation, the gun may have to change ammunition types to suit particular targets or situations, again firing a prodigious number of rounds. Missile systems are not suited to this task. Bearing in mind the fact that 8000 rounds of shell were fired in support of land forces during the Falklands operation, it will be seen that missile systems do not offer a good solution to the need for NGS. This is an area in which the medium calibre gun is unbeatable.

The amphibious force's most critical operation, that of moving from the ship to shore, will usually be undertaken in situations whereby the only fire support available is that supplied by the naval gun. The role of the medium calibre gun can be summarised therefore as providing the necessary fire power for:

> Advance force operations
> Amphibious raids and landings before shore artillery is established
> Flanking operations
> Covering amphibious forces during withdrawals after shore artillery has been
>   re-embarked
> Supplementing shore based artillery fire

Ideally, naval gunfire ammunition stocks could be used to resupply shore based artillery, however, in the absence of a ballistics agreement enabling ammunition to be interchanged, logistics will preclude this.

3

The Influence of New Technology

Weapons are shaped in response to operational requirements, which are statements of what the Navy needs, and by technology, which governs what can be achieved. Frequently, new technology makes possible new weapon capabilities and so stimulates new requirements, when the naval users see that something new can be done. Since technology is usually the dominant factor in the shaping of weapons, it is therefore relevant to look broadly at the whole field of weapons technology in order to see which are the principal thrusts of new technology that have been most responsible for the main advances in the naval surface weapons of today.

Weapon technology may be grouped under the general headings of Guns, Missiles, Information Technology and System Architecture, thus conveniently dividing the naval surface weapon field into the relevant blocks in which it is influential. Underlying all these areas are advances in materials and components. These provide the elements of new capabilities, whilst the extremely important influence of advances in electronics pervades all the weapon areas. New steels, plastics and composites contribute to an upward trend in weapon capability, but new electronic and electro-optic techniques contribute enormously to increased intelligence in weapons and sensors through the acquisition and processing of data. This is probably the most significant type of advance in the tactical application of both defensive and offensive weapons. So, while the military use of information technology may be seen as the strongest influence in the advancement of weapons, it must, at the same time, be appreciated that the requirement is for hardened and rugged equipment of which the components have been specially developed to operate in the extremes of shock, vibration, temperature and humidity—problems not encountered in most civil applications. Advances in software techniques, and mainly in real time software, are not so tangible but they have been of the greatest significance in modern naval weapons for which software control and automation are a necessary and increasing feature. Software design is changing from an art to a science and requires a new and precise, yet flexible, language for the weapon designer to use and express his requirements to a machine or system.

NAVAL GUN TECHNOLOGY

The technology of naval gun systems has made considerable strides. It is of interest to consider the medium calibre gun field where the views of Vickers Shipbuilding and

Engineering Limited are pertinent and are naturally linked with developments in Army guns.

Technological developments in the medium calibre naval gun field can generally be categorised into three spheres of activity; munitions, propulsion and gun systems design and control.

Munitions

Of all the advances in gun technology, those with the most far-reaching consequences are developments in the guidance of projectiles and in warhead design. Ideally, once fired a projectile should become autonomous and able to seek its target, identify it and attack it without further instruction from the platform or mounting that fired it. Autonomous projectiles, termed 'fire and forget', that carry a powerful explosive payload and deliver it with pin-point accuracy have far reaching and dramatic consequences. These systems are more expensive than ballistic shells and, as such, may not be in widespread use until the next century, but they are in cost competition with missiles and will probably replace some of these.

Various techniques for guidance are available, using either laser guidance or laser illumination of the target. A semi-active laser guidance system is used in the *Copperhead* artillery shell programme. However, in early trials of such guidance systems, although effective in dust and smoke, they would only work about half the time in the weather conditions typical of a winter's day in the North Atlantic. This problem has now been resolved. However, the difficulty of getting outside sources of laser illumination or laser designators to illuminate targets at a projectile's maximum range obviously poses restrictions on the system unless a remotely piloted vehicle (RPV) is used. Furthermore, such projectiles, because of their size and sensitivity, are difficult to handle in an automated system.

New generation systems include a 'fire and forget' shell with its own autonomous target acquisition and discrimination systems, using imaging infra-red, millimetre-wave radar or optical seekers. Such advances, provided that they are coupled with improvements in range, could form the basis of a gun system to engage strong armoured formations well beyond the forward edge of the battle area, and could be capable of attacking interdiction targets, such as roads, railway bridges and airfields. The precision guided shell would give the defender deadly stopping power. Yet however 'smart' these projectiles are, their development will depend on hardened packaged microelectronics and microprocessors to analyse, almost instantaneously the data which the guidance systems collect.

Effective software for such systems that would dramatically reduce the scale of latent defects in the programs and improve the overall reliability of the system has yet to be developed. To this end, two prime areas of development in medium calibre gun technology can be identified. One is the design and mass production of rugged microelectronic components of smaller size, packing more processing power into a given space. The technology is known as 'Very Large-Scale Integration' (VLSI). The other is the creation of 'fifth generation' computers using VLSI technology. The major difficulties of making such critical military computer systems lie in defining the degree of required reliability and ruggedness and in designing tests to ensure that the standards have been met, and in hardening computers against electro-magnetic pulse (EMP) effects from nuclear attack.

Sub-munitions, extended range shells and bomblets are available, enabling a single projectile to carry a number of small sub-munitions each of which is able to carry out a separate attack or to contribute to the effectiveness of a single hit. Guided sub-munitions using 'smart' projectiles, provided the technology is successful, should be able to engage many types of enemy formations in a short time. Each sub-munition, if it were a 'smart' projectile would scan the area with its own scanner and seek out a radar reflective target, and, under terminal guidance, attack the target. If a mix of projectiles was available, an amalgam of sub-munitions could be fired, giving an area attack whilst the next projectile could commence a point 'smart' attack on a specific enemy target.

This ammunition technology, if fully developed, will confer a greater probability of first time kill. Additionally, it will allow the engagement of moving targets to take place even though the target may start moving after the projectile has left the gun.

Most current guns are no longer manned and so can be reduced in size whilst requiring only environmental protection, using composite materials such as GRP. This also gives the benefit of reducing the radar signature. Other gun parts can be manufactured of light alloys and composite, again reducing weight and so enabling higher acceleration speeds in training and elevation to be achieved. Ideally, the gun must be made more intelligent, with the range table calculations and prediction and local reference at the gun.

Installation should be made simpler, demanding a modular fit. Instantaneous selection of special munitions to suit the action conditions and targets to be engaged should be possible. As stated above, gun control will, however, depend on the processors to be used in the system, particularly when smart ammunition is to be handled, if reliable selective ammunition delivery is to be achieved.

Propulsion

Since kinetic energy is a function of the square of velocity and the mass of the projectile, high velocities are vital and advanced propulsion methods are being investigated. These range from electromagnetic and electro-thermal methods of firing, as a long term aim, to liquid propulsion by the late 1990s.

Two liquid propellant projectile propulsion concepts are being developed, mainly for small calibre Army applications; the Bulk Loaded Liquid Propellant Gun (BLPG) and the Regenerative Liquid Propellant Gun (RLPG). In the BLPG system, liquid propellant is either loaded directly into the gun chamber or pre-loaded in a case. Because of difficulties stemming from controlling the ignition and combustion in the BLPG system, attention is focussing on the RLPG whereby the propellant is pumped directly into a propellant reservoir, which is separated from the chamber by a regenerative piston. The piston injects the propellant into the chamber during the combustion cycle. The system improves on conventional gun propellants in terms of internal ballistics, reduced barrel wear, reduction of flash and blast, temperature sensitivity and susceptibility to detonation if hit by enemy fire. Reduced stowage and logistic requirements coupled with financial savings in propellant production also make the system attractive. Interior ballistic calculations indicate that a 20 percent increase in muzzle velocity for acceleration sensitive projectiles is possible by using a RLPG system.

Base-bleed projectiles have been trialled on the Vickers 4.5 Mark 8 Naval gun mounting and the performance far exceeds that of the conventional shell. Ranges in excess of 60 kilometres are being investigated for Army artillery and this should apply to naval guns too. The base-bleed technique involves a pyrotechnic attachment to the end of a shell which burns for some 70 percent of the flight of the shell. This smooths out the turbulence behind the projectile and very greatly reduces the drag, thus giving a much greater range to the shell.

Rocket assisted projectiles, another area of development, will increase range without the need for large calibre or a heavier payload. Combined with terminal guidance, this ammunition gives an extremely high degree of accuracy.

To ensure that the small numbers of medium calibre guns required by individual navies can be financially worthwhile, future production would be more economic if undertaken on a collaborative multi-national basis. Standardisation of calibre and ballistics to reduce logistic costs and the initial procurement costs of the guns and ammunition would be very advantageous, as is widely recognised in NATO circles. The threats to naval vessels are thought to be becoming more similar to those for land based forces. Commonality with army services, using similar Ballistics Agreements, would be beneficial for naval guns. Single shot kill probability could be enhanced by carrier projectiles with submunitions, and by smart munitions fired from lighter, simpler and more reliable systems. This is a sound development using modern technology which, if properly applied, will ensure the medium calibre naval gun remains a very cost effective all-round weapon.

The fast firing naval gun systems which are totally automatic are dependent on software and data processing to enable them to select valid targets and reject others. Automatic operation is becoming an increasing feature of naval weapons as the speed of engagements increases. The sophisticated software involved is essential in this development, where it has made a major contribution.

As discussed above, precision guided munitions are made possible by having small rugged sensors in a shell which can receive guidance commands, and by having lasers or suitable millimetre wave illuminators to point with precision at the target. Here again, data processing is necessary in very small spaces and so the credit for making guided shells practicable must really go to electronics. Even more dependent on modern rugged electronics are self-sufficient, target-seeking shells.

Very dense, hard material is used in ammunition for 'penetrators'. These are sharp darts employed to pierce enemy missiles and explode their warheads. Tungsten and depleted uranium are used to provide the highest possible concentration of specific energy at the point of contact so that the armour protection of missile warheads may be penetrated.

Viewing all these characteristics of present day naval guns in perspective, two appear to stand out as truly significant technical achievements. These are the precision guided munitions (PGM), which enormously increase the accuracy of a gun against moving targets in particular, and the very fast firing, automatic target selecting guns giving three to four thousand rounds per minute and thus a greatly increased lethality, especially with penetrators. An extremely high standard of mechanical engineering and reliability is required and is achieved in the fast firing guns. The fact that this concept is practicable is a great triumph of clever engineering which should not be overlooked.

The ammunition costs of ballistic and guided shells are considerably lower than those of even the simplest missiles. Thus, with the object of gaining lower absolute cost, with adequate effectiveness, the technology drive to improve naval guns is now firmly established and very sensible. The naval gun is thus enjoying a return to popularity after being in the shadow of the missile for the last twenty years. The hybrid form of missile and PGM seen in the Shorts' Seastreak is a particularly interesting utilisation of modern technology as it gives much lower ammunition cost than a missile and a good performance in lethality; it may well be the first of a new type of low cost naval surface weapon.

NAVAL MISSILE TECHNOLOGY

It is interesting that the sea-skimming missile, which is probably the most significant naval weapon of modern times, does not utilise any great advance in technology to achieve its success through flying very low over the sea. It uses a radio altimeter to keep its height low, and while these are effective devices they are certainly not at the forefront of technology. It was the appreciation that a very low flying missile would be difficult to detect which was the key to their success. The actual achievement of low flight was not particularly difficult.

Missiles gain their advantages from speed, agility, a multiple launch capability and the intelligence to recognise valid targets and ignore decoys. Their velocity is derived from the form of propulsion used, and a singular technological achievement in this field is to have solid fuel motors which allow the missile to be easily handled and stored like a round of gun ammunition. In general, greater range is obtainable from liquid fuelled motors but the ranges of up to several tens of kilometres obtained from practical solid fuel motors are consistent with the horizon-limited range of shipborne sensors used to detect the targets in tactical engagements. So solid fuel missiles are both convenient to handle and quite adequate in range for most naval purposes. For the longer tactical ranges, turbines using kerosene are common and these are stored and handled in a fully fuelled state.

Missile agility is extremely important and more positive methods than purely aerodynamic control from vanes have been developed to enable the missiles to turn quickly through large angles in order to facilitate in-flight manoeuvres or rapid and radical turns on launching. Best known of these methods is thrust vector control whereby the output jet from the rocket motor, which provides the thrust, is delivered out through one or more nozzles which can be swivelled typically through 10–15 degrees. This technique provides a strong impetus to change the direction of the missile quickly and through a wide angle at slow as well as fast speeds. Another method, used by Aerospatiale, is to employ gas jet thrusters near the centre of gravity of the missile to push it rapidly in different directions. One form of agility, giving the missile a pre-programmed weaving course, makes it more difficult to hit. In the same way, agility in an anti-missile missile increases its effectiveness against weaving targets. The current trend in attacking ships with missiles is to use the technique of saturation. The attacker fires a number of missiles simultaneously or in a 'ripple' or stream, closely spaced and, if possible, from different directions, in order to saturate the defence. To counter this, the ship needs to have a number of channels of fire which it can control separately. Point defence missiles fired from conventional launchers were really intended to provide one channel of fire per launcher and were linked to a directing radar which was not good enough for saturation attacks, especially if the radar was also limited to directing one missile at a time.

To overcome these problems vertical launching was conceived. A large number— say thirty—missiles are stacked vertically in launching containers and can be fired in groups with each missile, ideally, being capable of being allocated to a separate target and homing to that target independently. Vertical launch clearly requires a high degree of missile agility to turn it over after launch in the direction of its allocated target, and here thrust vector control is important. Vertical launching also eliminates the blind spots which can occur when a conventional trainable launcher is obstructed on some bearing arcs by the ship's superstructure. The technology involved in developing and testing vertically launched missiles is complex and in the case of VL *Seawolf* a special trials barge named *Longbow* is used by British Aerospace.

The barge is used in conjunction with the missile firing range at Aberporth. A six-point mooring system has been provided in Cardigan Bay to which *Longbow* is towed for trial firings. The barge is maintained on the required heading for the trial, with a limit of ten degrees, by use of two power winches in the stern and two 720 horse-power diesel engines, which drive two Schottel propellors and other machinery. In addition, the draught can be altered by up to two metres by the filling or blowing of two ballast tanks to assist with the alignment of radars and the establishment of trials parameters. A helicopter landing pad in the stern allows missiles to be flown out before each trial. *Longbow* has its own surveillance radar and meets full Board of Trade and Lloyd's standards. It was refitted for a life of at least 10 years.

108 metres long with a beam of 30 metres, the barge's length equates to that of a frigate. It is equipped with two launcher frames, one forward and one aft, to hold VL *Seawolf* missiles in their launch cannisters, of which each frame can hold three. A Type 911 tracker radar, part of the VL *Seawolf* weapon system, is mounted upon a superstructure amidships. The disposition of the radar in relation to the launch cannisters, including height above sea level, is the same as is to be provided in the design of the Royal Navy's new Type 23 Frigate (*Drake* class). (These will be the first ships in the Royal Navy to be equipped with VL *Seawolf* systems. Each will carry launcher racks for 32 missiles.) High speed cameras, positioned beside each launcher, record the flight of the missiles as they are fired. An area of about 30 metres square below the upper deck is known as 'the citadel'. This houses all the launch control, trials recording and ship-to-shore communications equipment. Before firing, these systems are synchronised with the land-based trials equipment at Aberporth so that comprehensive correlated records of each trial firing are obtained. Trials and telemetry data are relayed in real time from the barge to Aberporth range control over a secure communication link.

The *Longbow* barge is shown in Figure 3.1 and a sequence in the firing of a VL *Seawolf* is shown in Figure 3.2 where the first photograph shows the shattering of the frangible cover over the canister and later pictures show the efflux being vented vertically, followed by the emerging missile.

Probably the most significant influence of technology on modern missiles is the provision of intelligence in their heads to enable them to navigate complex courses

Fig. 3.1   Vertical Trials Barge *Longbow*. (*Photo: British Aerospace*)

and then to detect and select viable targets and discriminate against false targets. This is a contribution from electronics and software which enables a considerable degree of intelligence to be packaged into a very small space. Missiles can now use more than one sensor, e.g. radar and infra-red, to look at targets and they can be 'told' quite fully what a valid target looks like. They analyse the target characteristics, which they see, and compare the results with information in their memories. As a result, modern missiles are very difficult to deceive with simple decoys. The advent of the microprocessor, with its associated memory, greatly increases a missile's capability. A very good example is the Cruise missile, with its navigation ability over long distances. Complex flight plans can now be programmed into a sea skimmer so that, in a mass attack, missiles can arrive at the target ship from a number of different directions at virtually the same time. The addition of electronic intelligence makes the greatest contribution of all to the formidable capability of the modern naval missile.

FIG. 3.2   A sequence in the vertical launching of Seawolf. (*Photo: British Aerospace*)

INFORMATION TECHNOLOGY

Just as data processing and software have made major contributions to the intelligence of missiles, so has information technology had a dramatic effect upon naval weapon systems as a whole, and particularly upon their sensors. Information technology has had an enormous effect in civil applications of all kinds including banking, finance, accountancy, the stowage of records, business management and even typing. It is still being applied more widely and continues to grow in significance. However, in the defence field it faces a much more demanding and hostile environment as well as a wide range of potential applications. The processors and the solid state components must operate in greater extremes of temperature, humidity, shock and vibration. Hence, understandably, the pace of growth of information technology has been slower in defence than in civil fields. Even so, there are two basic reasons why naval (and other defence) weapon systems must have a wide use of information technology. The quantity of data from new and improved sensors, as well as the data needed to control weapons, is now much too great to be processed by men, and the speed at which all this data must be processed and assessed, due to the extremely short time of engagements, is much too fast for them. In consequence, larger command systems are now a vital part of every significant warship with the assessment and processing of tactical data being carried out in a distributed manner at each sensor and weapon as well as centrally in the ship's Action Information Organisation.

This digitised process is now quite essential. A warship involves a number of paths of data flow throughout its interior which are an absolutely necessary means of exercising command and control over its weapons and sensors. To facilitate this, the digital data highway has been a most important development. This is basically a transmission line or loop using concentric cable or glass fibre with adaptors or terminals on it through which equipments may be connected. Data, addressed to the terminal it is intended for, is passed along the highway and is extracted only by the appropriate terminal. Thus information is continuously being passed in both directions, between terminals, and the data highway is akin to the system of arteries and veins in a body in its significance. It is duplicated several times in different parts of the hull and superstructure so that if the ship is damaged there is a chance that one of the data highways will survive.

If any of the equipments attached to the data highway are damaged or inoperative, the highway and its flow of data are not affected because the highway does not go 'through' the equipments, they are merely attached to it. Thus the lifeline of the warship's tactical data flow is really independent of the weapons and sensors; it allows for what is known as 'graceful degradation' in the event of equipment failure or damage and, with its own multiple redundancy, it ensures a high degree of security to the flow of tactical data. While it does feature extensively in the detailed design of individual displays, sensors and weapons, the overall processing, distribution and assessment of tactical data in a warship by digital methods is the main contribution of new information technology.

NAVAL WEAPON SYSTEM ARCHITECTURE

System architecture is the manner in which individual equipments, such as guns, missiles, radars, data displays and electronic warfare units, are linked together and

FIG. 3.3 Bofors 57 millimetre Mark 2 dual-purpose gun on board the Swedish coastal corvette Stockholm. This class also carries the Bofors 40 millimetre L/70 aft and the RB15 missile system. (*Photo: AB Bofors/Naval Forces*)

used collectively to provide overall weapon capabilities. The aim is broadly to achieve better performance in lethality, reaction time and effectiveness, but it can also yield economy through the use of the separate equipments in a more flexible and versatile way for more than one purpose. System design is difficult and complex. It is, potentially, a powerful factor in obtaining weapon effectiveness and economy in relation to the operational tasks which are required of the ship. With such a large array of weapons and sensors now available as building blocks, the problem of which to select and how best to use them is understandably important. Computer-based modelling of engagements is used to evaluate different combinations which have been indicated as potentially suitable by theoretical assessment.

The weapon system in a warship should provide a balanced capability so that even if the ship has a special purpose, it will also have a chance of defending itself from other forms of attack. The weapon system design should also aim at the lowest absolute cost consistent with its task and this may lead to a concept of modularity where equipment modules may be used for more than one purpose, as in the Contraves *Seaguard*. This is primarily a CIWS incorporating a fast firing gun and the necessary radar and electro-optic sensors and data processors to control it using a data highway. But all the equipments are designed as separate modules so that they can be sited in the most appropriate places in the ship and can also be used to control large and medium calibre guns, surface-to-air missiles and electronic warfare decoys and helicopters as well as providing general radar surveillance for the ship. This concept gets the most value from equipments and leads to low absolute weapon system costs.

Seaguard was designed as a modular, rather than a unitary 'all in one system'. Thus each module is small and light enough to operate with the necessary dynamic performance to meet the threat in terms of:

> Reaction time
> Shifting target immediately the engaged target is destroyed in a stream attack
> Tracking and engaging targets at or near the zenith
> Tracking and engaging close range targets with high horizontal and vertical crossing rates. (Whole ship length protection and continuous engagement of manoeuvring targets—both horizontal manoeuvre and vertical 'bunt' weapons)

But modularity has other significant advantages:

> Each module can be sited where it should be to extract maximum operational effectiveness:
> (1) *Search radar antenna* at the truck of the mast
> (2) *Trackers* high in the ship with clear arcs of vision
> (3) *Guns* low down in the ship with a close range capability against sea skimmers and optimal weight destribution
> Multi-sensor tracking is made possible by separating the tracker from the gun.
> Electro-optic sensors are rendered inoperable by gun flash, smoke and outgoing projectiles if the gun and tracker are co-located.
> Mutual interference is avoided between the gun and other system components which could arise from vibration, tracking lead angles and interacting torques.
> Each system can be tailored to meet the exact and most cost effective requirement of the client navy in numbers of search radars, tracking modules and guns for each ship.
> Components can be integrated with the other ship's systems—particularly the search radar which provides a good general purpose medium range surface and air search radar as well as navigation radar for the ship, and tracking modules which can provide a good tracking quality for control of all ships weapons in AA, surface and NGS roles.

The modern approach of using a distributed processing system can be employed, thus:

> The configuration of the system is flexible
> There is growth and modernisation potential
> There is never a danger of exceeding processing capacity
> Redundancy is provided within the system

Full uninterrupted hemispherical tracking and engagement can be provided by *Seaguard* to cope with both sea skimmers and vertical diving missiles while the ship is rolling and pitching in bad weather. In addition to fire control and CIWS capability, *Seaguard* also incorporates a total weapon control AIO Combat System if required.

The operational significance of this type of system architecture is considerable. In any 'hot war' scenario which involves a multiple missile attack, the most immediate problem to be faced by the defending force is weapon saturation. The surface forces being attacked run out of weapons to allocate to targets long before they lose capacity in sensors, command or EW capability. The advantage of a modular system like *Seaguard* is that, under such conditions, it makes optimum use of every weapon which is available in that it duplicates the control element and also allows the allocation of more than one weapon at a time to each tracker. It increases the numbers of tracking channels available, which improves the engagement capacity, and so makes a significant contribution to overall weapon effectiveness.

The economic significance of weapon system modularity may be dealt with under two headings:

First, cost effectiveness, which is always difficult to quantify with realistic accuracy and generally depends on value judgements.

However, even allowing for this, the quality of performance and flexibility of deployment and employment of the *Seaguard* system is an important factor when comparing modular with stand-alone systems.

Second, and this can be quantified better, is absolute capital cost. Here modularity makes a singular contribution because, once it has been decided how much equipment is required to ensure survival, a modular system allows the fitting of only those components required to meet the requirement, while at the same time reducing the numbers of equipment modules needed to achieve this because of the versatility, flexibility and multi-role capability provided by each individual module. In the field of defence, where costs are generally rising at a rate in excess of inflation and probably faster than in any other field of endeavour, such a contribution is of extreme importance. Put more simply, it means that economies are achieved by using equipment units for more than one purpose.

Weapon system design for multiple channels of fire within the layered air defence concept, using vertical launching of missiles and CIWS guns, is important to counter saturation attacks. All this, together with the other surface and underwater weapons, must be orchestrated and controlled within the overall ship weapon system including its data highways, action information organisation and command system of data processors. Clearly, the design of such an assembly, aided by modelling, simulation, trials, theoretical assessment and much operational experience is of cardinal importance.

Weapon system architecture is at the top end of the scale of sophistication in the field of ship weapons and it is one of the most important contributions to naval warfare which is made by a combination of technology and naval operational experience. With such a wealth of naval weapon capability now available from the supply industry, the problems facing the warship designer are more those of choice than those of invention. Weapon system design, for economy and effectiveness, is now emerging as a new technical subject which the leading weapon manufacturers are developing to complement and guide their traditional task of making individual weapons and sensors.

FIG. 3.4   HMS *Illustrious* fitted with Vulcan Phalanx guns fore and aft and Sea Dart
surface-to-air missiles. (*Photo: Crown copyright*)

Somewhat remarkably, naval surface weapons are not at present being strongly
influenced technologically by new means of achieving greater explosive and destructive power, but rather by data processing and software to gain intelligence in the
weapons and by the organisation of their use in ships. The sea-skimming missile
represents really the most significant advance in modern times in naval offensive
weapons, and this is, in fact, a triumph of the *concept* of concealment from detection
rather than a major achievement in using a radio altimeter to gain a low flight profile.
It is thus not so much a triumph of a new technological advance as a triumph of
weapon system thinking. It represents a masterly appreciation of what would defeat,
or severely test, the existing design of weapon systems in ships, embracing radar
sensors, guns, missiles and, particularly, the data handling and command processes
which were previously much too slow in operation to react in time to a sudden,
short-range threat. The sea-skimmer is, in this sense, a prime example of the
importance of system thinking in offensive naval surface weapons. It also illustrates
well the importance of the system concept in selecting the defensive weapons needed
for a ship to counter a threat which demands that the entire sequence of events must
be considered and provided for in the *system* of sensors, software and weapons.

From the necessarily limited number of selected aspects of technological influence
on naval surface weapons discussed in this chapter, it is, hopefully, clear that the
dominant factors are not primarily those relating to more destructive power, but
more those relating to weapon intelligence, system design and lower cost. In the
technologically rich climate we now enjoy, the problems are not so much those of the
invention of new weapons as those of choice, organisation and cost.

4

Naval Guns and Guided Projectiles

Naval guns are the most traditional type of weapon for surface warships. As we have seen they are at present being accorded more priority and importance as naval weapons after a period in which they tended to be replaced in larger ships of frigate size and above by missiles. The Type 22 frigate of the Royal Navy was hailed as its first all-missile ship, but one of the lessons of the Falklands War was that a number of air threats, especially in confined waters, were better dealt with by guns. The fitting of guns is now much more widespread in all navies to give ships more of a complete, self-contained defence capability. Typically, naval gunfire support for land operations is provided by guns of a calibre of 4.5″ to 6″ and current views on naval operations now favour specialised gun systems for this purpose, thus restoring the important role that gun systems used to enjoy.

To economise on naval armament by fitting a 'general purpose' medium calibre gun is, in many quarters, no longer an acceptable policy and specialised guns are now being widely fitted. Some of these, known as Close-In Weapon Systems, form the innermost ring of the layered air defence concept against missiles and aircraft discussed in Chapter 2. These gun systems have a very high rate of fire of up to 4200 rounds per minute, are totally automatic in operation and possess great sophistication in software and in mechanical design. They acquire and select their own targets, and engage them in the range bracket of 1000 to 2000 metres; they represent a magnificent contribution of modern technology to gun system design and performance from software, electronics and mechanical engineering. Other specialised gun systems guide the shells to the target to increase lethality in one of the most advanced aspects of gun system design. While there is a wide range of naval guns and gun systems available now from the weapon supply industry it is convenient to review these in four categories:

> *General purpose*, manually operated 20 to 35 mm calibre guns for air and surface targets at short range for general tactical and policing duties.
> *Larger guns* of 4.5″ to 6″ calibre for naval gunfire support and surface targets.
> *Close-in weapon systems* with a very high rate of fire and fully automatic operation to counter anti-ship missiles and aircraft.
> *Gun system firing guided projectiles.*

and we will consider illustrative examples of weapons of these types.

GENERAL PURPOSE MANUALLY OPERATED GUNS

There will always be a need for a simple, relatively low cost naval gun for general purpose and policing duties. Such guns may be the main armament in very small ships or the secondary or tertiary armament on larger ones (Corvettes, Offshore Patrol Vessels, Destroyers, even Aircraft Carriers). Whatever their intended fit, these weapons must be easy to install, operate and maintain, and they must be powerful.

Excellent examples of this type of gun are produced by the Oerlikon company and widely used by many navies including the Royal Navy. The A41A is the lightest and simplest gun in the Oerlikon naval range. It mounts the well-proven HS 804 cannon which gives the gun a rate of fire of 800 rpm at a muzzle velocity (mv) of approximately 850 metres/sec. The on-mount ammunition capacity is 58 rounds, contained in a quick exchange drum magazine. The gun is exceptionally light (225 kg with a full drum) and has very low recoil forces (3.6 kn). With a swept muzzle radius of only 1.7 metres, it can be fitted in very small patrol craft and motor boats. It is shown in Figure 4.1 and is really the simplest type of 20 mm calibre naval gun, with a range of some 1500 m.

The GAM B01 is Oerlikon's prime general purpose 20 mm naval gun. It uses the Oerlikon 20 mm KAA cannon and ammunition and is probably the most powerful conventional 20 mm weapon on the market. This gives effective performance against surface targets out to 2000 m and against air targets to 1500 m.

The key features are:

High rate of fire: 1000 rounds per minute on automatic or, if selected, single shot.

High muzzle velocity of 1100 to 1150 metres/sec giving an almost flat trajectory to 1000 metres.

Powerful ammunition.

200 rounds of belted ammunition in a front magazine which can easily be changed by two men, either from the side or front. A hand tool is supplied for splicing in fresh belts of 25 rounds during a pause in the action.

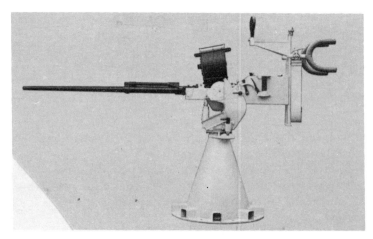

Fig. 4.1   Oerlikon 20 millimetre A41A gun. The simplest form of naval armament. (*Photo: Oerlikon*)

A crew of only 2 men—1 × Aimer
                             1 × Loader/Lookout.

The mounting is constructed of aluminium alloy to reduce corrosion and for lightness. The total weight of the gun complete with 200 rounds of belted ammunition is 500 kg.

The gun is rugged and simple, and efficient gun crews can be trained in 5 days, without previous knowledge. 300 of these guns are at sea. Over 100 have been bought by the Royal Navy since June 1982 and are fitted now to most surface ships in the British Fleet.

To provide really effective naval AA defence, it is of course necessary to provide weapons with a higher rate of fire, more powerful ammunition and more precise fire control than is available from simple manually operated 20 mm guns.

To meet this requirement, Oerlikon have produced a range of twin 30 and 35 mm dedicated naval AA guns, all capable of being controlled by any modern digital or analogue fire control system.

The GCM AO3 gun has a rate of fire of 1300 rounds per minute from two cannon, ie, 22 rounds a second.

For law enforcement purposes, the gun can also be set to fire single shot and to conserve ammunition during practice shoots, it can be set to fire repeated single shot at 90 rounds per minute.

The high automatic rate of fire combined with the gun's accuracy arising from a combination of high mv, the barrel steady and tight servo performance have proven on trials at sea that the gun has an accuracy of 3 milli radians at 3000 metres when controlled by a modern fire control system. The effective range in local control will be somewhat reduced by poor visibility and approximations in the gyro gunsight's prediction of lead angle.

The deck must be strong enough to support the gun which weighs about two and a half tons with a maximum recoil force of 32 kn. Deck stiffness should preferably be above 25 Hz. Lower values are acceptable only if the damping factor is high enough to prevent the excessive transfer of recoil energy into the deck.

The gun does not penetrate the weather deck. Put in another way, it does not require gunbay space between decks for on-mount ammunition or control equipment—a very positive asset if being retrofitted. It is simply bolted down by 16 bolts onto a base ring with a plinth high enough to take the slip ring connections and to ensure that the aimer's cab does not ground on spent cartridges. With a suitably installed base ring, it may be fitted in a few hours. Fire Control System integration can take a further 3–5 days. The gun is seen in Figure 4.2. A wide variety of ammunition is available, from inexpensive target practice rounds to high explosive incendiary and armour piercing rounds with tracer.

To destroy modern, heavily armoured, close support aircraft, Oerlikon have developed a new fragmentation HEI shell (high explosive, incendiary). This has a slightly thicker and tougher shell case than the HEI but almost the same explosive filling. The fuze is in the base to ensure correct functioning inside the target, be it a ground support aircraft or helicopter.

The APDS-T, standing for Armour Piercing Discarding Sabot with Tracer, consists of a sub-calibre penetrator made of exceptionally dense metal, for example

FIG. 4.2   Oerlikon 30 millimetre Anti-Aircraft Gun GCM AO3. (*Photo: Oerlikon*)

a tungsten alloy. All the power of the propellant is transmitted via a pushing disc to this small sub calibre solid bullet which is guided up the barrel by plastic sabots which are discarded on leaving the muzzle. The penetrator itself has a fairly snub nose for punching its way through the armoured targets. It is, therefore, provided with an aluminium ballistic cap for streamlining in flight. The cap melts on impact with the target and lubricates the passage of the penetrator.

It is not thought by Oerlikon to be cost effective to fit Proximity (VT) fuzes to shells under 76 mm. The fragments have insufficient energy to cause enough damage to prevent an aircraft returning to base. A high kill probability through direct hits resulting from a high rate of fire, high muzzle velocity, tight auto-follow and lethal ammunition is considered a better design aim.

Automatic Gun OE/OTO 35 mm

Moving up the scale of performance and sophistication in this class of gun system is a twin based 35 mm gun provided by Oto Melara which is a very good example of the more automatic mounting which is available today.

The OE/OTO 35 mm is a small calibre twin naval mounting designed and developed for use on any type of warship down to motor-gunboats. Due to its compactness and limited weight, the mounting can also be installed aboard merchant ships of any tonnage as local defence during wartime. It is primarily intended for anti-aircraft and anti-missile point defence with a secondary anti-ship role. The guns are the 35 mm Oerlikon KDA 35/90.

The gun mounting characteristics are as follows:

Light weight and small overall dimensions;

Fast reaction time;

A high rate of fire: 1100 rds/min (550 rounds per barrel);

A large number of rounds ready to be fired (800).

Manoeuvrability and readiness to fire against closing high speed air targets even in rough sea conditions;

Unmanned operation, with the mount loaded;

A dual feed system for each gun to fire two different types of ammunition: anti-aircraft or armour piercing, with remote control selection;

Protection against green water load ensured by the water-tight fibreglass shield;

A solid state electronic control system;

Easy maintenance and repair due to the accessibility of the components and the use of modular sub-assemblies.

This gun is a fully automatic, remote controlled weapon. The two Oerlikon KDA 35/90 guns and a twin ammunition feeding automatic system are mounted on the carriage. The carriage and feeding system constitute a single assembly training on a single bearing.

The Oerlikon 35 mm KDA machine gun is a gas-operated weapon. The feeding system consists of two containers for the ammunition belts and two booster-assisted conveyor ducts, one for each gun. With the mount completely fed, about 800 rounds can be fired without the intervention of personnel. The mount is remote controlled: any manual operation is excluded in normal conditions. The train and elevation servo-systems are electrical with solid state controls using silicon controlled rectifiers. The motors have low inertia printed rotors. The feeding, loading and firing systems are hydraulically operated by a hydraulic power unit fitted on the lower shank.

Both guns are provided with a muzzle velocity measuring device which continuously feeds back the muzzle velocity information into the FCS computer. Each weapon has, on the elevating mass, a magazine for 20 rounds of armour piercing ammunition. The selection time of the ammunition to be fired is two seconds.

The gun can fire the following ammunition:

High explosive incendiary shells with self destruction fuze, for anti-aircraft and missile close defence;

Armour piercing, high explosive incendiary shells with a bottom fuze, for use against lightly armoured targets;

Armour piercing, subcalibre hard core shell with discarding sabot, specifically developed for use against heavily armoured targets;

Practice shells with tracer.

The gun is used with a separate sight at the remote control position and the constituent parts of the mounting are shown in the cut-away diagram in Figure 4.3.

The mechanical design of fast firing guns of this type is most impressive and the high reliability they achieve is a tribute to the thoroughness of their development.

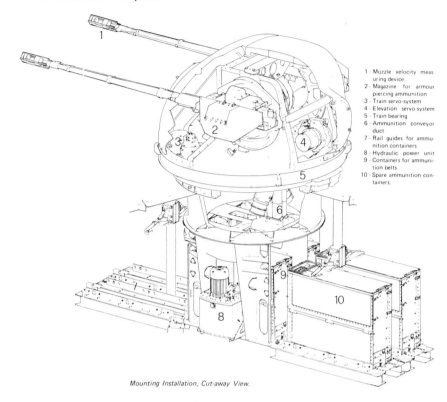

1 · Muzzle velocity meas-
  uring device.
2 · Magazine for armour
  piercing ammunition
3 · Train servo-system
4 · Elevation servo-system
5 · Train bearing
6 · Ammunition conveyor
  duct
7 · Rail guides for ammu-
  nition containers
8 · Hydraulic power unit
9 · Containers for ammunition belts
10 · Spare ammunition containers.

Mounting Installation, Cut-away View.

FIG. 4.3   Oto Melara 35 millimetre twin gun. (*Photo: Oto Melara*)

LARGER CALIBRE NAVAL GUNS

For naval gunfire support through shore bombardment out to ranges of some 23 kilometres, for engaging surface targets and for a measure of point defence against aircraft and missiles there are two guns which admirably illustrate this class of surface weapon: the Ota Melara 5″ known as the 127/54 Compact and the Vickers 4.5″ MK 8. Both guns use fire control sensors of radar or electro-optics to obtain target range, bearing and elevation information which is fed into the gun control units but we shall be concerned here primarily with the actual weapons.

The 127/54 Oto Compact

The 127/54 Oto Compact is a dual purpose, rapid fire, 5 inch gun mount intended as main armament for frigates and destroyers. In consequence of its reduced weight and compact configuration, it is possibly suitable for a wider category of warships than other guns of the same calibre and the same rate of fire. It is claimed to provide the ship with an effective and reliable point defence against high speed attacking aircraft or missiles and an effective shore bombardment and anti-ship capability.

The mount is fully remote controlled with automatic loading of 66 ready-to-fire rounds held in three loader drums. Each loader drum, with a capacity of 22 rounds, can contain different ammunition, so that three different types of rounds can be available for immediate fire. Switching from one type of ammunition to another requires only about seven seconds before the new ammunition is fired. The loader drums are automatically fed, even with the gun in operation, through two hoists manually loaded in the ammunition magazine.

The installation can be considered in three parts: the turret, installed on deck, the automatic feed system, installed below the weather deck, and the two lower hoists entering the ammunition magazine.

The turret holds the elevating mass, the gun loading system and the train and elevation mechanisms.

The gun loading system consists of two loading trays, two radial arms mounted symmetrically to the elevating mass and a round transfer mechanism.

The automatic feed system comprises the three loader drums and an upper hoist taking the round transfer mechanism on the mounting. The gun loading system and the automatic feed system are hydraulically operated and electrically controlled. Rounds are taken from the drums and hoisted to the elevating mass in a series of short movements thus reducing acceleration on the moving parts and the round itself.

The two lower hoists transfer the rounds from the ammunition magazines to the three loader drums. The rounds are lifted step by step by means of a transfer chain and in the upper position are automatically positioned on the loader drums by two transfer trays.

The gun system is completed by a *control console* at which the gun captain pre-sets the mount for operation, selects the type of round to be fired, monitors the mount operation, controls barrel cooling and setting for maintenance work. The mount is fitted with servo-systems of very light weight, with plug-in modular electronics and identical train and elevation drive motors, three for elevation and eight for training.

With remote control, the gun can be readily laid onto all presently foreseeable targets and retained in lay under all operational sea conditions. Aiming response rates of the servo-system are fast and the mount is capable of very high training and elevation speeds ensuring accurate fire at all firing rates.

The feeding and loading systems are hydraulically operated through four self-contained hydraulic power units, two on-mount and two off-mount. Firing rates are selectable between 10 rounds per minute minimum to 45 rounds per minute maximum.

All available types of 5 inch calibre ammunition can be fed, loaded, fuzed and fired without adjustment to the mount. Misfires are automatically ejected thus permitting rapid clearing. The training arc is 330 degrees and connection with off-mount components is through torsion cables. Tracking is continuous with the intervention of an obstacle contouring device and firing cut out cams. An inverse slewing device is provided.

A large use of aluminium alloys reduces the mount weight to 34 tons. The shield is made of moulded fibreglass and is watertight with complete protection against nuclear fall-out. Its anti-icing features and internal temperature controls allow all-weather operations, withstanding green seas, very high speed winds and the most severe temperature conditions. The mount operates unmanned. Reloading of the loader drums can be accomplished by 4 to 8 handlers in the ship's ammunition magazine. The gun captain at the control console near the automatic feed system performs the mount switching and pre-setting for operation.

The mounting for this major gun is shown in Figure 4.4 where the internal structure can be seen. There are two loader hoists transferring the rounds (projectile and cartridge) one by one from the ammunition room to the automatic feed system. They are of the vertical chain type, with a step by step chain movement which is continuous in both directions of movement. Each hoist consists of a lower station (feeding station), an intermediate duct section and an upper station.

The lower station is contained in the ammunition room. Onto this station the cartridge and the projectile are introduced separately by the gun crew. A normal crew of ammunition handlers of 2 to 4 men is required for each hoist, according to the rate of fire to be used in sustained fire. No watch routine is required for the ammunition handlers.

The intermediate duct section connects the feeding station to the upper station, forming a guide for the rounds during their travel. The length of the duct section depends on the on-board installation of the mount.

The upper station is arranged on the platform of the ammunition feed system and forms the terminal part of the lower hoist. It includes a transfer tray. The rounds in this station are drawn by the transfer tray and positioned vertically (projectile and cartridge at the same time) in a loader drum. A transfer tray serves two loader drums. The drum to be fed is selected by the operator at the control console.

The 127/54 Oto Compact fires semi-fixed ammunition ensuring the projectile has a muzzle velocity of up to 807 metres per second and a range of 23.6 kilometres for an angle of elevation of 45 degrees.

The projectiles fired, having the same characteristics and weights, are of the following types:

> Disruptive HE (High Explosive), high fragmentation projectiles fitted either with percussion or mechanical time fuzes;
> Disruptive HE (High Explosive), high fragmentation projectiles fitted with a proximity fuze;
> Practice round with inert projectile.

Percussion fuzes operate very quickly with point detonating and graze action. A delayed arming clockwork mechanism provides a trajectory safety of not less than 100 metres. Mechanical-time fuze operation is based on a clockwork principle. A safety disk prevents functioning of the fuze at less than 1.5 seconds of flight. A minimum calibration setting of 2 seconds is provided. Proximity fuzes are self-powered, radio-pulse, transmitting and receiving units, primarily intended for use against aircraft, sea skimmer and diving missiles.

Projectiles, filled with A3 compound (RDX with 9 percent of wax), weight approx 31.7 kg including the fuze, with the charge accounting for 3.57 kg. The propelling charge is contained in a brass cartridge case. The charge is a single base, seven hole diphenylamine powder with stabiliser and anti-flash additive (SPDF type). The weight of propellant varies from approximately 8.1 to 8.4 kg. The primer is the electric type. The complete round weighs 47.9 kg. The projectile overall length is 665 mm with a cartridge overall length of 834.5 mm.

Cartridges are packed in individual air- and water-proof metal containers which ensure storage, transport and handling safety conditions. Projectiles are packed in

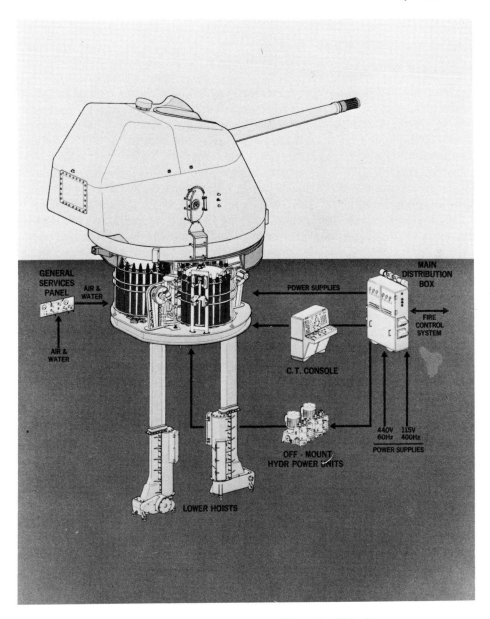

FIG. 4.4   127/54 OTO Compact Gun. (*Photo: Oto Melara*)

wooden boxes with the fuze protected by a steel nose cap and driving band with a fibre grommet.

The Vickers 4.5″ MK 8 Naval Gun

The Vickers 4.5″ MK 8 naval gun is extremely well known in naval circles throughout the world. It was developed to meet the needs of the Royal Navy in close co-operation with the United Kingdom Ministry of Defence and it provides all the high standards of engineering and accuracy required of a weapon to operate reliably in extreme conditions on ships down to 800 tons displacement.

The design of the 4.5 MK 8 is aimed at complementing other ship defensive systems but, more importantly, it provides a warship with a weapon that has an operational capability for naval gunfire support, surface fire, air defence and patrol and policing.

Entering service in 1973 on HMS *Bristol*, the 4.5 MK 8 naval gun has since matured into a weapon that has gained much respect world wide. Operational in 10 classes of warship and serving in six navies, it has established itself as an extremely versatile and reliable weapon. On numerous occasions in multi-national exercises the 4.5 Mark 8 has demonstrated the advantages of having long range and high accuracy, coupled with well-developed ammunition.

While exercises are useful yardsticks by which a weapon's performance can be judged, the only real test is in battle and the 4.5 MK 8 is truly combat proven.

Its versatility has been well demonstrated in successful operations against land, sea and air targets including extensive action in the Falklands War.

The gun is a remotely controlled fully-automatic single mounting developed for a general purpose role in a wide variety of warships, giving a rate of fire of 25 rounds per minute.

The mounting includes a rotating turret enclosed by a lightweight gunshield moulded in a glass reinforced plastic which gives protection against extreme weather conditions and low energy shrapnel. The turret houses the on-mounting feed system and the gun barrel. Below the turret is the gunbay area in which fixed ammunition is stockpiled in the feed system in readiness for transfer up the centre pivot hoist to the gun. The ammunition feed system is powered hydraulically and controlled by a logic system to ensure safe operation at all times. Ammunition, once introduced into the system in the gun bay, is then handled automatically through a number of simple transfer operations. An autoloader puts the ammunition onto a rotating feedring which then delivers it to a two-stage hoist for transfer on the on-mounting feed system. A pivoting loading arm raises the ammunition to the gun where a rammer loads the breech to complete the loading cycle. Spent cartridge cases are ejected from the system through trunking onto the weather deck.

The nature of the ammunition being fired can be changed quickly without disturbing the stockpile of ammunition on the feedring. For example, starshell can be fired at a few seconds' notice before reverting to normal operation. Continuous operation of the mounting at the specified rate of fire of 25 rounds per minute can be obtained with only two loaders transferring ammunition from the ready-use stowages to the gun system.

All ammunition for the 4.5 MK 8 Naval Gun is fixed. Each round is individually packed in self stacking containers which ensures that they are fully protected from

FIG. 4.5   Vickers 4.5 inch Mark 8 Naval Gun fitted to a destroyer of the Royal Navy.
(*Photo: Vickers Armstrong*)

damage during embarkation and need not be handled until required for loading into the feed system.

Besides a completely inert round, which is used for non-firing drills, there is a total of five types of ammunition available for:

High effect, designed to cause maximum fragmentation and blast damage with its 2.5 kg of high explosive.

Illumination providing a mean output of 600,000 candelas for a 40 second period at a descent rate of 4 m/sc.

Radar echo shells are available in two frequency ranges, I and J band; this chaff round can be used as a passive decoy or for wind finding.

Anti aircraft practice rounds have a small flash filling which permits visual verification of fuze functioning.

Surface practice rounds use a completely inert shell and fuze for surface target practice.

Two types of fuze are used with 4.5 MK 8 ammunition.

> *A time fuze* is used with the illuminating and HE rounds, and is mechanically set by hand to give the required time of flight.
>
> *A multi-role fuze*, designed to match the characteristics of the HE shell fragmentation pattern, is also fitted to the AA practice round. A choice of four roles is available and setting is carried out electrically immediately prior to loading the gun.

Roles 1 — *Direct Action*   — to explode on impact

2 — *VT Low*
3 — *VT High* } promixity settings which cause the shell to explode within pre-determined distances from the target

4 — *Post Impact Delay* — to a explode at a pre-set time after impact.

In a naval gunfire support rôle, the gun has exceeded all expectations both in the hands of the Royal and overseas navies. Its range of 22 kilometres and extremely high order of accuracy enable it to take up a stand-off bombardment position, beyond the range of defending forces, and lay down a devastating bombardment. When linked through forward observers, it is possible to achieve consistent pin-point precision against individual targets.

Again, the long range and high accuracy which is achieved, coupled with a highly lethal shell, provides the 4.5 MK 8 with the capability of inflicting crippling damage on surface vessels. Even at night and in poor weather conditions, it has not been deterred from its mission to engage and destroy. The introduction of post impact delay fuze setting adds yet another dimension to its destructive capability. The consequences of a HE round entering a target ship's compartments before bursting into over 3000 high velocity fragments will have a devastating effect.

A good performance in the AA role is achieved due to a combination of the large radius of influence of the shell when fuzed in the VT high mode and the speed and accuracy with which it can be delivered even when engaging at long range.

One of the most difficult engagement scenarios to consider is against the sea skimming missile. Trials against this target are claimed to have been highly successful.

In-depth computer simulations of engagement, with a variety of air targets, have shown that the 4.5 MK 8 Naval Gun has an overall capability against such targets comparable with other smaller calibre high fire rate guns.

The Lince System

For gun direction of any gun system under difficult conditions when the target is very low or radars cannot be used due to jamming or a radio silence policy, modern methods employ electro-optics and lasers for ranging out to distances in excess of 15 kilometres for surface targets, eight kilometres for aircraft and four kilometres for missiles. One such director is the Lince (Laser Improved Naval Combat Equipment) made by Oto Melara. As well as a laser for ranging, it uses daylight TV, low light TV or infra-red cameras for target tracking and these can, of course, operate down to very low angles of elevation at which radar could not be effective.

The Lince System can operate in two main modes:

Completely automatic, where the target is tracked by the tracker system which, processing the video signal, keeps the line of sight continuously on target; range data are automatically provided by the laser rangefinder.

Semi-automatic or manual (back-up mode) where manual tracking is through a joystick or tracking ball; Range with relevant spotting corrections is entered through hand controls and lead angles and ballistic corrections through pedals.

In both modes of operation, firing is obtained through direct operator action on a firing pedal.

Acquisition and angular tracking are made possible by the application of contrast technique to the image of the target against its background, as viewed by a high resolution camera (TV or IR). Range data are achieved by means of a high repetition frequency laser rangefinder.

Calculation of automatic kinematic lead angles and ballistic functions is achieved through the use of a hybrid computer, employing micro-computing techniques, operating on the target geometrical and kinematic data, and on the projectile and meteorological data. Range and lateral spotting correction introduction (only when firing against surface or shore targets) is possible through operator intervention.

The firing computer gives the elevation and bearing lead angles in the form of synchro signals for directing the gun.

Manned by a single operator, this system can perform the following operations:

Surveillance against surface and low air targets.

Target designation acceptance from external designation sources such as radar or TV.

Target acquisition and tracking by an optronic camera system.

Automatic tracking (angular and range) with TV tracker and Laser range finder.

Manual rate-aided tracking (angular and range) with a joystick or tracking ball.

Line of fire calculation for air and surface targets.

Introduction of range and lateral spotting corrections.

Complete control of one light medium calibre gun or control of two guns of the same calibre.

Kill and damage assessment.

This system is a typical example of the use of modern electro-optical technology in present day gun systems and it strongly reinforces the use of radar for gun direction.

CLOSE-IN WEAPON SYSTEMS

These constitute the inner ring of layered defence and they are, in fact, the 'last ditch' active defence of a ship against missiles or aircraft which have 'leaked' through the outer layers in mass or saturation attacks. Electronic warfare decoys can be included in this inner ring too, but they are not active elements of defence.

The CIWS problem for the future is to provide an effective kill probability against a supersonic sea skimmer with a speed of about 700 metres/sec, which is more than double that of current missiles, with an armoured warhead. Destruction must be effected at a range where the missile fragments are not likely to damage the ship. At present, the safe minimum range for hitting sub-sonic missiles is thought to be 1000 metres, which represents less than two seconds before an undamaged supersonic missile would hit the ship. One method used is to employ very hard and sharp 'penetrators' in the shells which must make a direct hit on the missile and explode its warhead at a safe range from the ship. A direct hit on an approaching sea skimmer is difficult. Not only is the radar cross section very small—about 0.35 or 0.40 metres in diameter—but also the missile will not fly a straight path, due to air turbulence and the nature of the guidance system, which cannot smooth out the course into a perfectly straight line. Indeed, it may be programmed to make a complex approach. Radar tracking will meet with the 'glint' problem.

If a hit is achieved, the penetrator rod has to pass through all the obstacles in the front assembly without being deflected, hit the warhead front plate at a good angle, and still retain enough specific kinetic energy to pass through this into the payload and cause a chemical reaction, detonation or deflagration.

The useful cross section for this purpose will be much less than the 0.35 or 0.40 metres referred to above since, beyond a certain angle of incidence, the penetrator will glance off. It is clear that, velocities being equal, the lighter the penetrator the more likely this is to happen.

There is also the factor that the uncertain reaction time of high explosives is such that a chemical reaction does not always follow even where the requisite kinetic energy values are present. Three or four hits may be required. It is questionable whether the very brief combat time available, combined with tracking problems, allows for three or four hits on the same warhead, let alone in the same place, on that warhead. Larger calibre shells with bigger penetrators may offer more effectiveness even though the rate of fire is lower.

Missile destruction may also be attempted by the use of proximity fuzed ammunition where the object is to damage the guidance system by proximity activated bursts of many pre-fragmented shells at ranges of 3000 to 1000 metres. This might not actually destroy the missile but it could put it off course and significantly increase its miss probability, provided it is achieved at sufficiently long range. Otherwise, the damaged missile could simply continue on its ballistic course and hit the ship.

It is relatively easy to defend a missile against frontal hits from a small calibre shell, since the main requirement is the addition of steel to protect the warhead. To protect the missile against penetration into the flanks by pre-fragmented proximity-fuzed ammunition would require armour plating the whole missile. Since the missile would than become much heavier and larger, it would require more propellant and strengthening of its rudder servos and fins. It is estimated that the total effect of all this could be to add 400/600 Kg to the weight of the missile which would about double the cost, and make the missile less versatile in use.

So, the problem for the CIWS of a fast firing gun is quite formidable and the extent to which it has been overcome by the gun system designers in industry is very impressive. The Breda 'Fast Forty' Twin Naval Moinotiring fires 900 40 mm rounds per minute, some rounds being proximity fuzed and pre-fragmented for use when the target is at longer ranges. This ammunition is changed automatically to direct hit penetrators when the target reaches a range of 1000 metres. At this range the direct hit probability of the shell is higher and proximity fuzed fragments would not be so effective. This gun system, with its radar director is, of course, totally automatic in acquiring and engaging its targets unless inhibited by a human operator.

FIG. 4.6   The Breda Fast Forty CIWS. (*Photo: Breda*)

The gun is shown in Figure 4.6 and its ammunition arrangements in Figure 4.7 where the upper magazine houses the penetrator rounds and the lower magazine houses the proximity fuzed rounds.

The associated servo system is designed with fully digital technology and is controlled by a high performance processor, specifically developed for this application, which is characterised by high speed computation and a large memory capacity.

The servo motors employed are dc, and identical for training and for elevation.

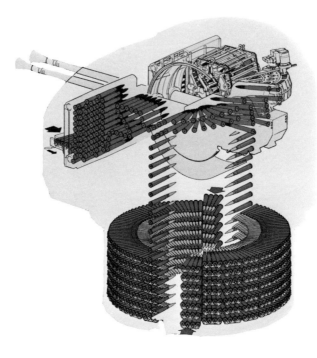

Fig. 4.7   Breda Fast Forty magazines. (*Photo: Breda*)

Instead of the conventional synchro control transformers, encoders are employed, one fitted to each, to transmit the feedback signals (relative to the position of the gun) in digital form to the amplifier.

Apart from improvement in servotechnical performance, in terms of training accuracy and shorter slewing time, digital technology applied to the servo system presents other special characteristics:

> Control of the gun by means of serial transmission of gun orders through a two wire cable.
> Easy and fast introduction of prohibited zones by means of a keyboard.
> Rapid alignment of gun and the fire control system.
> Automatic correction of line of fire in relation to platform inclination.
> Display of diagnostic messages on the Local Control Panel.

The result has been to combine the two anti-missile gun-kill philosophies of fragmentation and penetration by designing a new Breda recoiling mass, redesigning the mounting for dual ammunition feed and taking advantage of new penetrator ammunition generating higher specific kenetic energy.

The intention is to provide a defence against anti-ship missiles when they become supersonic with a more heavily protected warhead, and a weapon equipped to meet saturation attacks more successfully, by an all-round AA gun. This gun would also be capable of defence against light craft, having ample space for any type of 40 mm ammunition with almost 1000 rounds on each mounting.

In the 30 mm calibre there is a lighter weight system provided by Breda. *Sea Cobra* is the name of this new Close-In Weapon System in which a Marconi 440 series radar is installed in the Twin 30 mm Mounting, with the radar director mounted on top of a gunhouse designed for this purpose, and with the transmitter/receiver, signal processing and data extraction units installed inside the gunhouse. The operational control console is a separate unit, connected to the gun via slip rings. The design allows scanning at 60 rpm to acquire radially approaching targets. Once tracking has been established, the gun is slewed to the target bearing, the aim off is injected, and the gun is ready to fire. This self-acquisition sequence minimises the reaction time to an incoming threat. Alternatively, the system responds to target co-ordinates designated for engagement by the AIO or CIC. The mounting is controlled through the transmission of serial data and data transmission is bi-directional. Data transmitted to the mounting from the fire control system consist of training and elevation position data and control command logic. Data transmitted from the mounting consist of present position data and logic signals of mounting status—out of alignment and inhibited zones. While similar in principle, the performance of *Sea Cobra* is less than that of the *Fast Forty* but it is suitable for fitting on much smaller ships.

At the upper end of the scale of performance and sophistication in close-in weapon systems is the *Goalkeeper* system provided jointly by Hollandse Signaalapparaten BV (Signaal) of The Netherlands and the General Electric Company (GE) of the United States. This provides a rate of fire of 4200 rounds per minute of 30 mm shells from seven barrels and is a totally integrated, self-contained, fully automatic system designed for any close air target be it a missile or an aircraft in the presence of an EW environment.

Goalkeeper is an autonomous and completely automatic weapon system for short-range defence of ships against highly manoeuvrable missiles and aircraft. The system automatically performs the entire process from surveillance and detection to destruction, including selection of the next priority target. However, manual override is possible at any stage in the sequence. The crucial importance of a last-ditch defence system has been proven on numerous occasions. To provide for this need, Signaal developed *Goalkeeper*, which is an extremely effective system, that has already found its way to several navies.

Goalkeeper incorporates the General Electric 30 mm, seven-barrel GAU-8A Gatling gun. The combination of Missile Piercing Discarding Sabot (MPDS) ammunition and a firing rate of 4200 rds/min gives the system the power necessary to destroy missile warheads. The magazine capacity is sufficient to permit successful engagement of several targets under worst-case conditions before reloading. Search and tracking radar, weapon control and integration of the total system are the responsibility of Signaal. A high detection probability for small targets is ensured in all weather conditions by the use of a high-power, coherent, pulse-to-pulse I-band search radar. A synthesizer-driven Travelling-Wave-Tube (TWT) transmitter permits great frequency flexibility, which augments anti-clutter and ECCM performance. Pin-point target tracking is achieved by the dual frequency I/K band tracking radar.

The system features automatic target indication. Threat priority is determined automatically and is immediately followed by automatic direction of the tracking antenna to the 'priority one' target. Continuous search with track-while-scan ensures rapid engagement of the next priority target in multi-target scenarios.

Mount, gun, and search and tracking radars are integrated into one fast, devastating system.

Goalkeeper has a high detection capability by autodetection and target acquisition at ranges which allow plenty of time for target engagement. This should be the prime requirement that any weapon system of this kind has to meet. Through *Goalkeeper*, detection of small targets is ensured under all weather conditions by the use of the I-band high-power search radar with its high data rate.

I-band offers an optimum balance between excellent target reflection, low lobing effect and deep atmospheric penetration. A synthesizer-driven travelling wave tube (TWT) transmitter provides high power for burnthrough and permits great flexibility in frequency and prf to counteract jamming. The antenna speed of 60 rpm ensures a high data rate for immediate detection of pop-up and fast manoeuvring targets. An elevation beam of 60 degrees, bi-axially stabilised, assures continuous track update, independent of the ship's movements. Advanced processing techniques, such as digital pulse compression and FFT (Fast Fourier Transformation), guarantee detection of very small targets in dense clutter environment. Digital Moving Target Detection (MTD) is incorporated for unambiguous range indication under clutter conditions. *Goalkeeper*'s pulse repetition frequency stagger and frequency diversity are valuable anti-clutter and ECCM features, additionally avoiding blind-speeds. The threat evaluation and target designation module automatically determines threat priority and initiates target engagement by software. Continuous search enables fast engagement of subsequent targets in a multi-target scenario. Detection is followed by rapid designation and acquisition by the tracking radar. Dual frequency I- and K-band tracking has been chosen, a technique patented by Signaal. Over 150 systems using this principle are currently in operation. The K-band pencil beam produces a small resolution cell, providing accurate and continuous tracking data at very low target altitudes. Sustained, automatic comparison of the signal-to-noise ratios of the I- and K-band returns ensures uninterrupted tracking in a degraded environment. Anti-clutter and ECCM features also guarantee accurate tracking under all conditions at sea. Automatic optronic tracking by TV (or as an option by IR) is also provided.

Curved-path prediction filters are used accurately to predict the hitting point. Local measures of heave and acceleration avoid false target movements being recorded. Automatic calibration and closed-loop hitting point correction serve to compensate random bias errors and environmental factors. Manual override is possible at any stage in the sequence of operations.

The gun has a very high firing rate of 4200 rounds/minute, and a low dispersion. 1190 rounds of ready ammunition are stored in the ammunition feed-and-storage drum. This enables several targets to be engaged successively before reloading. Spent cases are returned to the drum to avoid above-deck debris.

The below-deck location of the feed-and-storage drum provides a protected environment for reloading. Reloading can be accomplished with a manual loading tray or, if desired, mechanically with the rapid bulk loading system. Over 650 GAU-8/A gun and feed systems have been produced for the United States Air Force A-10 aircraft. With over 10 million rounds fired, the gun has demonstrated a cumulative reliability of more than 150,000 Mean Rounds Between Stoppages (MRBS) which is very impressive. The GAU-8/A gun permits prolonged fire bursts

FIG. 4.8   Goalkeeper CIWS showing the radars and the guns. (*Photo: Hollandse Signaalapparaten BV (Signaal)*)

of eight seconds to handle multi-target situations with proven reliability and precision.

Goalkeeper's operational ammunition is a 30 mm Armour Piercing Discarding Sabot (APDS) round. The projectile contains a high-density tungsten alloy penetrator, and embodies the lethality needed against current and future missile threats. Its terminal effectiveness ensures warhead kills. For soft targets and training purposes, mass-produced low-cost HEI and TP ammunition is available. The kill assessment enables immediate engagement of a series of targets at short intervals. In all respects, *Goalkeeper* offers a balanced system approach.

The complete system is shown in Figure 4.8. The gun can fire at an elevation of 80 degrees and in depression to 20 degrees below the horizontal level. Great sophistication lies in the software associated with the selection of viable targets and with the ordering of these into threat priorities. Altogether *Goalkeeper* is a prime example of the state of evolution of modern CIWS and an excellent illustration of the growing trend of software control and total automation in naval surface weapons.

The anti-ship missile is undoubtedly the greatest threat to naval units today. When approaching at wavetop level, it is capable of penetrating a ship's outer defences unnoticed, and can cause extensive damage. In the light of the importance of a ship's mission, the value of the crew and the ship itself, the protection afforded by the *Goalkeeper* system is clearly very significant.

Finally, the *Seaguard* system produced by the Contraves Company in conjunction with Plessey is probably technically the most interesting and significant CIWS because it is designed to do much more through the use of the modularity principle. In this method of system design its sensors, processors and displays can be used for other purposes, and so provide a potential for economy in the total weapon system of the ship. As well as providing an automatic, fast-fixing CIWS gun, it can also control EW decoys, a medium calibre gun, a point defence missile, an anti-ship missile and helicopters as well as providing a measure of AIO facilities. It is an excellent example of the flexible and economic use of equipment units which is likely to be an important future trend in overall ship weapon system design. It brings forward for examination the degree of simultaneous use of all these capabilities which might be needed in future conflicts involving saturation attacks. In conjunction with Plessey and Oerlikon a family of equipment modules has been assembled which includes:

A C-band, high and low elevation, anti-missile and general air and surface surveillance and target indication Search Radar Module.

A 3-axis, Ku-band Radar Tracking Module with fully integrated, electro/optical line of sight optimized for tracking of Mach 3 plus, sea skimming and high diving missiles, inclusive of an operator console.

A 25 mm quadruple, anti-missile and anti-aircraft Gun Module using high energy, armour-piercing rounds with a rate of fire of 3400 rounds per minute.

A 3-axis, X-band Radar Tracking Module with fully integrated, electro/optical line of sight optionally with an integrated CW illumination capability to guide semi-active homing missiles, and an operator console.

A Command and Control Module using one or several NAUTIC tactical consoles for command executive decisions both for the deployment of *Seaguard* and other weapon systems on board.

A Common Support Module as entry port for data between any *Seaguard* configuration and other equipment on the ship.

A Weapon Control Module for interface, ballistic and prediction computation for any selected type of gun, or for missile system interface and control.

The search radar module is a dual beam-C-band Radar for surveillance, detection and target indication of missile targets as well as general air and surface targets in severe environmental and ECM conditions. The common support module (CSM) provides the track processing of the search radar output. A navigation mode is integrated into the main operating modes of the radar and made available to the CIC. Optionally, a dual rotation rate is available to increase the long range capability of this radar.

The Ku-Band tracking module is a 3-axis multi-sensor (Ku-band Radar, FLIR, Laser) tracker mounting for highly accurate target tracking throughout the hemisphere and with high dynamics for rapid reaction and engagement of close-in high speed targets. The multi-sensor concept of this tracking module enables very low-level tracking of sea-skimming targets as well as targets approaching from throughout the hemisphere around the ship, and in a dense ECM environment. The X-Band tracking module is a 3-axis multi-sensor (X-band Radar, TV or FLIR, Laser) tracking mount for highly accurate long range target tracking throughout the hemisphere and with high dynamics for rapid reaction and engagement of high-speed

Fig. 4.9   The Seaguard System. (*Photo: Contraves*)

targets. The multi-sensor concept of this tracking module provides high redundancy and makes this line-of-sight impervious to ECM and multipath effects when very low flying targets are being tracked. The tracking radar is equipped with a second range gate for differential tracking and can be equipped optionally with CW injection for target illumination.

The tracker and weapon control console is manned by one operator and equipped with a 10 inch PPI display, TV data display, TV FLIR picture monitor, keyboard and joystick. The tracker and weapon control console is part of the Ku-band tracking module as well as the X-band tracking module, and provides for the detailed monitoring of the *Seaguard* engagement sequences and control of the Seaguard search radar module.

The 25 mm Gun Module is a canted two-axis gun mount with four 25 mm Type KBB independent cannons having a rate of fire of 3,400 rounds per minute. The canted axis allows zenith and high angle engagement. A ready-use stock of approximately 1,700 rounds allows 20 engagements before the need to re-load. Topping-up of ammunition can be made without interruption to operational availability or, indeed, firing.

The command and control module is for overall command and control (AIO). It comprises one or more autonomous intelligent consoles linked by a command system highway. This module provides the command and control facilities for all ship roles and, in particular, situation assessment and weapon assignment. A key feature is the replicated data base in each console continuously updated through the highway. This modern naval system approach provides efficient operational teamwork and an unusually high level of redundancy in the event of battle damage or equipment failure.

Ship-to-*Seaguard* interfaces and *Seaguard* internal logistic functions as well as TWS and TEWA programs, are concentrated in the common support module. Except for logistic functions, most requirements in these areas change with customer and with *Seaguard* configuration. The outward appearance of the common support module can therefore change from a half size standard *Seaguard* electronics cabinet up to two or more full size cabinets.

The weapon control module fulfils several functions related to the type of weapon which is controlled. The heart of the weapon control module is a *Seaguard* processor which permits interfacing a particular weapon with the *Seaguard* digital bus. Normally the weapon control module is a full size standard *Seaguard* electronics cabinet.

This system effectively provides total hemispherical CIWS defence. The gun can fire vertically upwards and all round the hemisphere, and the command and control facilities will either act as a complete AIO for small ships or as an addition to the AIO in large ships. However, the key feature in the system design concept is the potential for economy through the use of the modules for several purposes in weapon control.

The dominant design criteria for the *Seaguard* family of modules was the achievement of the required performance against anti-ship missiles under the constraints of cost and ease of installation. Each module is therefore the result of careful analysis of the options available to defeat the missile threat as a result of which the adaptation of existing anti-aircraft equipment was rejected, due to failure to meet the exceptionally demanding performance requirement against missiles. Therefore an approach was selected which took the available technological base to design a new family of modules needed to configure an optimized CIWS and which also included the elements to satisfy the requirements of classic fire control and command system functions. A key decision in the feasibility studies of *Seaguard* was the decision to select either a modular or integrated concept of equipment. The predominant reason for *Seaguard* being modular is that only by the application of this concept can the necessary performance against missiles be achieved both now and in the future. Modularity allows, among other advantages, the unique zenith capability and the achievement in the CIWS of extremely high tracker and gun dynamics necessary to engage very high speed targets at very close range and to defend the whole length of the warship. In the case of surface and air defence gun control, this concept allows integration of different types of weapons already on board a ship, and can thus combine them in a layered defence philosophy in which an approaching target is dealt with successively by different weapons, each in its own optimum range bracket.

The *Seaguard* system uses dedicated processors distributed to their point of use and linked by a digital data bus. This permits each processor to be dedicated to one particular task to maximize the utilization of its computing power and avoiding the problems of a centralized computer.

Thus no two *Seaguard* systems will be alike, they will always be tailored to meet specific customer requirements, interfaces with other equipment at different levels and the constraints dictated by the type or class of ship into which they are fitted. At one end of the scale, it is a total Ship's Combat System while at the other it can be a two module CIWS. In between these two extremes, it can be fitted and interfaced at any level as desired by the customer to include surface-to-air missiles. EW decoys and general purpose gun fire control or AIO facilities as needed.

FIG. 4.10   Seaguard's guns firing vertically. (*Photo: Contraves*)

Seaguard can be fitted in a wide range of ships from fast attack craft to frigates and aircraft carriers and in terms of system design concepts it provides a way ahead for naval surface weapons which could lead to lower absolute costs of total weapon systems. The system is illustrated in Figure 4.9 and the guns firing vertically upward are shown dramatically in Figure 4.10.

GUIDED PROJECTILES

To improve the accuracy of guns against moving targets, and particularly against aircraft and missiles, techniques have been developed to provide means of correcting the course of a shell in flight if the movement of the target after the shell is fired is such that a hit is unlikely. Such weapon systems are sometimes known as Precision Guided Munitions (PGM) though there is no universally agreed definition of this term.

The basic reason for this development is cost; over the last 40 years guided missiles have been developed to improve the accuracy of purely ballistic projectiles. While they certainly did so, the cost per round compared with that of a shell was vastly increased. Now the objective is to retain the basic shell fired from a gun but to provide some means of altering its course after firing in response to a movement or manoeuvre of the target. The cost of the new shell will be increased but it will still be a lot less expensive than a missile and, if the accuracy and lethality are significantly better, the overall result is a more cost-effective weapon. The first PGM to enter service recently was the 155 mm calibre *Copperhead*, and others are now in development. The early PGMs used a semi-active laser system. In this concept, it will be remembered, the target is illuminated by a laser from the firing position and the reflected laser signal is received by the shell and used to generate guidance commands in the final stage of the ballistic trajectory. The laser illuminator need not necessarily be at the firing point but can be elsewhere with a forward observer. In ship systems it is, however, likely to be on the ship firing the shells. Lasers and infra-red guidance systems are influenced by cloud, mist and rain so that millimetric radar at around 94 GHz may well have a better all-weather capability. Guidance can also be obtained by using command systems where the position of the shell and target are monitored by a radar sensor at the firing position and a command is sent to the shell to activate a change of course. This is a more economic method, as the cost of the shell is minimised and the main complexity of signal processing is confined to the shipborne equipment. Command systems will be used for the smaller calibre shells, where space is limited. The control techniques for the shells include moving fins and tail vanes as employed in guided missiles, but thrusters and impulsers using explosives or pyrotechnics are also used to change the course of the shell.

In collaboration with Oto Melara, British Aerospace is designing a course-corrected shell for the Oto Melara 76/62 (3 in) rapid-fire naval gun to destroy manoeuvring air targets—primarily sea-skimming anti-ship missiles.

British Aerospace is developing the weapon fire control and guidance system which assesses the corrections needed to the shell's trajectory to ensure it intercepts its target. Course correction commands are relayed to the shell which responds by varying its flight path. Detonation of the shell is triggered on impact, or by proximity fuze. Course-corrected shells will enable the Oto Melara 76 mm calibre gun to engage and destroy small manoeuvring air targets, such as anti-ship missiles at greater ranges

Fig. 4.11   A cut-away diagram of the Oto Melara 76 millimetre Super Rapid gun and an illustration of it fitted in one of the Hong Kong patrol craft. (*Oto Melara*)

and with greater certainty than the so called 'last ditch' multiple gun close-in weapon systems. Only minor modifications are required to the gun to enable it to fire these shells.

The basic design philosophy being adopted by Oto Melara and British Aerospace is to install as much of the guidance electronics as possible on board the ship to achieve an inexpensive 76 mm shell, some 15 to 20 times less costly than the cheapest of missiles for this task. The course correction will be made once, by detonating one of a number of small thruster charges mounted around the shell. In this system of course correction, the target is tracked by radar and the position of the projectile is calculated and predicted. If it seems that the projectile will miss the target, its course will be corrected to bring it close enough for the proximity fuze to operate. However, this task is not easy as the shell leaves the gun spinning at some 20,000 rotations per minute and at the moment of detonation of the thruster the orientation of the projectile must be known in order to determine which thruster to fire. So, flip-out stabilising fins are added to slow the rotation to about 200 rotations per minute and the firing signal for the thruster is transmitted as an electromagnetic wave linearly polarised at a certain angle. The angle of polarisation is sensed in the projectile and this information is used to fire the appropriate thruster. In effect the projectile does a direction finding operation to measure the angle of polarisation and so select the appropriate thruster.

This is clearly a complex technology. However, if the improvements in accuracy and lethality are good enough, the PGM is likely to play a major role in anti-missile point defence and possibly replace the point defence missile to a large extent.

The Oto Melara 76 mm Super Rapid gun will fire these guided projectiles at a rate of 120 per minute. Against any one target there may well be several projectiles in flight at once and so course computation for all of these will have to be done and coded signals sent to ensure that the right course correction is carried out by the right projectile. This will add to the signal processing task but it is well within the capability of modern processors.

The main components of this gun are shown in Figure 4.11. It is light enough at 7500 kg to be fitted in small hydrofoils and powerful enough to be the main gun on frigates. With a PGM capability against sea skimmers and aircraft it will be a very versatile and significant naval gun.

5

Anti-ship Missiles

Present-day anti-ship missiles employ the principle of sea-skimming whereby their guidance in the vertical plane is controlled by a radio altimeter which causes them to fly at a constant low height of a few units to a few tens of metres above the sea. The height can be pre-set in accordance with the prevailing sea state and wave height. The missile then steers itself to the target in the horizontal plane and may employ the sea skimming mode for all, or only the final phase, of its run. It is very difficult to detect by the target ship's radar and while it can be detected by ESM, if it is a radar homer, it may only use radar homing for the final few kilometres of its flight. This means that the target ship may have only 30 seconds or less warning of attack. This is a very short time in which to carry out such defensive measures as deploying EW decoys or bringing its defensive arrangements to bear. Automatic defensive measures are really essential.

The sea skimming anti-ship missile is thus an extremely potent naval weapon. Indeed it is undoubtedly the most significant factor in naval surface warfare in modern times. It has had a profound effect upon naval tactics and its effectiveness was dramatically shown in the Exocet attacks upon British ships in the Falklands War. Current missiles are sub-sonic, and while the next generation will be super-sonic the present missiles are not in any way lacking in effectiveness. At present the balance of effectiveness in attack and defence is heavily in favour of the attacking missile.

Some success in defence has been scored by simple chaff decoys, but new missile homing heads are likely to be able to discriminate against this form of decoy and the more sophisticated solutions of fast-firing guns, active off-board decoys and anti-missile missiles will be needed. The design of a weapon system of such high performance is not arrived at by merely combining various techniques in which the manufacturer possesses expertise; it is the answer to operational criteria that define both the system and its use.

The technical solutions to satisfy these criteria must be mutually coherent: the missile's overall operational effectiveness can be no greater than the least good of its separate qualities (efficacy of the warhead, accuracy, unobtrusiveness, reliability) just as outstanding performance in a particular area is an illusory advantage unless it is consistent with the other performance characteristics.

PENGUIN

The first anti-ship missile in the West came from the Norwegian firm Kongsberg and is named Penguin. Originally it was not a true sea-skimmer, as they are known today, but the latest version has this capability.

The Penguin anti-ship missile was conceived in the early 1960s as an anti-invasion defence system. It became operational in 1972 as the first fire-and-forget anti-ship missile system in the Western world. Since then, continuous development programmes have adapted the concept to the evolving technology of surface warfare.

The latest version, with folding wings, is presently being adapted to the SH-60B Seahawk helicopter in the US Navy's LAMPS III programme.

Penguin is a sub-sonic missile with canard control. The high resolution, passive infra-red seeker provides a high degree of discrimination and target selection, and ensures efficient operation in confined, as well as open, waters. The highly accurate inertial navigation system ensures the missile's capability of target selection and provides a measure of flexibility in the mid-course trajectory via an operator-designated waypoint. An efficient 120 kg warhead, with an impact point close to the target waterline, will inflict serious damage on medium-size surface combatants and other potential targets. The missile is powered by a solid-propellant rocket motor, which contains a booster and a sustainer motor, or a sustainer only when the missile is launched from a fighter aircraft.

The missile consists of common guidance and warhead sections, and an interchangeable motor and wing section for the various applications, thus enabling a common logistics system for all users. With a weight of only 380 kg, Penguin can be adapted to most weapon carriers. Its all-digital guidance and control system, with an internal data bus, facilitates integration with all modern fire-control systems. It can provide a common, efficient, stand-off anti-ship missile for a wide variety of platforms, such as large and small ships, land-based coastal defence systems, patrol aircraft, fighter aircraft and helicopters.

The ship-launched Penguin is now operational on 76 ships in four navies. With a maximum range matched to the surface radar coverage of the ship, and with the combination of passive operation and dog-leg manoeuvres, Penguin will provide small- and medium-size ships with an effective offensive weapon against most surface-ship targets. The short reaction time, and its very short minimum range, also make it suitable as a self-defence missile system for larger, high-value ships.

The low weight and low cost of the system make it cost effective to use a number of Penguin missiles in salvo firings for suppression of enemy missile defence, either as a stand-alone weapon system, or as a supplement to other long-range missile systems.

The different missile variants belong to two groups, the Mk2 and Mk3. The Mk2 family is adapted to stationary or slow-moving launching systems; ships, helicopters or mobile coastal defence systems. They all have an internal booster motor which accelerates the missile to its cruising speed. The Mk3 ASM is adapted to fighter aircraft. It has no booster motor, but a larger sustainer motor and a correspondingly greater range.

The ship-borne Penguin Mk2 system consists of five main units:

> Missile in its box launcher or transport container
> Missile control cabinet
> Operational panel
> Bridge firing panel
> Safety-arming unit

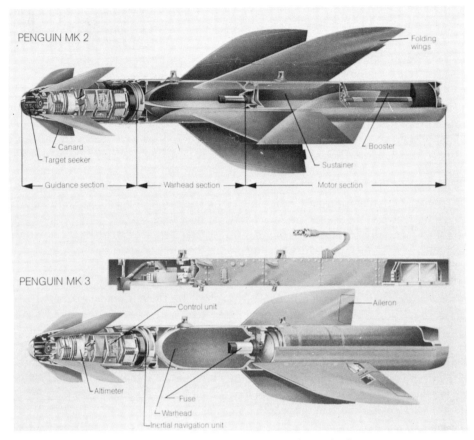

FIG. 5.1   Details of the Penguin Missile. (*Kongsberg*)

The weapon system will normally be operated from the Operation panel, which may be integrated in the ship's Fire Control System. At this panel the operator can select, start and check the missile, select single or salvo firing; straight or dogleg trajectories. In emergency situations, missiles may also be launched in a secondary mode through the bridge firing panel, which can operate independently of the fire control system.

The missile itself is of a conventional aerodynamic design, rolling airframe with cruciform wing configuration and canard fin control, and consists of 3 main sections; motor, warhead and guidance. The motor section contains a two-stage solid propellant rocket motor, i.e. a booster motor and the sustainer motor. The booster motor will accelerate the missile to its high subsonic cruising velocity, which will then be maintained throughout the flight by the sustainer motor. The warhead section contains the Bullpup Mk19 semi-armour piercing warhead with a charge of 50 kg HE. The fuze is an impact fuze with delayed action, to ensure that the warhead will penetrate the hull before detonation, in order to inflict maximum damage to the target. Controlled warhead tests within naval targets have shown that the warhead blast effect will cause very serious damage to almost total destruction within a radius of some metres. Thermal and fragmentation effects will be instrumental in damaging equipment and installations, and in causing secondary fires outside the primary blast area. As the missile impact point will normally be in the lower part of the target's hull, close to the waterline, the warhead will cause serious damage to targets up to destroyer size.

It is in the guidance section that we find the features which distinguish the Penguin from other known anti-ship missiles. The Penguin target seeker is a mechanically scanning passive infra-red (IR) system. However, in contrast to most infra-red systems, the Penguin IR seeker is a target seeker in the true sense of the word, and not only a tracker. It has the capability to search the target area autonomously, acquire and classify the target, and then change over from the search to a track mode.

When the missile approaches the target area, the seeker is activated, and starts searching a strip of the sea surface at a fixed distance ahead of the missile. Due to the very high manoeuvrability of the missile, this search distance can be kept very short, thus markedly reducing the influence of poor IR visibility upon the system performance.

When the seeker has detected an object that satisfies the decision criteria it automatically changes to its track-while-scan mode for the terminal guidance. In this mode, the seeker works as a pseudo-imaging system, mapping out the target contrast against the sea background, independent of possible target hot-spots. The seeker will then guide the missile to an impact point close to the target waterline, where the warhead can have its maximum efficiency. The all digital signal processing, together with other built-in features, is claimed to facilitate efficient schemes for discriminating between decoys and real targets, giving the seeker a very high resistance against IR countermeasures both in the search and track phases.

Furthermore, the weapon operator can select from a given set of shapes and image sizes which may be in the seeker field and instruct the seeker to disregard a certain number of targets. By tailoring the seeker operation to the actual tactical situation, it is thus possible to handle the more difficult cases of attacking a specific ship within a formation, or a target close to a land-mass, where certain radar systems may have difficulties. This advantage comes from the greater discrimination possible in IR compared with radar systems.

To utilize fully the different features of the IR seeker, the missile is equipped with a highly accurate digital autopilot and inertial navigation system, with the added unique capability of trajectory shaping. The inertial navigation system will guide the missile during its mid-course flight towards the computed target intercept point, either along a straight course, or following a right or left turn dog-leg trajectory. The navigation system also corrects for ship movements at the instant of launch, aim-offs up to ±50 degrees, and any cross-wind components that may be encountered during the mid-course flight. Level mid-course flight is also maintained by the height being updated by a pulsed laser altimeter.

Although the Penguin Mk3 is basically an adaptation of the Mk2 for use with the F-16 Air Combat Fighter, there are some important differences that should be pointed out.

The motor section is a single chamber, composite grain sustainer which will give the missile a range in excess of 40 km. The wing span has been reduced from 1.4 m to

1.0 m, while at the same time the wings have been equipped with ailerons for roll stabilization. The pulsed laser altimeter of the Mk2 has been replaced by a radar altimeter, which permits altitude control from high altitudes down to sea-skimming. The use of distributed microprocessors and internal data bus communication allows a high degree of flexibility in weapon system operation.

Whereas the Mk2 missile can be programmed to fly a straight course or dog-leg trajectory, the Mk3 can be programmed in both the horizontal and vertical plane to fly via a designated waypoint. The missile may, for instance, be launched from an aircraft over land, within 50 degrees off the aircraft heading, cruise out at a safe altitude for terrain clearance, descend to sea-skimming when over the sea, and turn in the direction of the designated target area.

The missile can communicate with the aircraft avionics through a bus system or dedicated wiring. In the case of the F-16 aircraft, all missile control and operation functions are by software integrated in the aircraft's original weapon control system, with no extra hardware installation.

The adaptation of Penguin Mk3 to the F-16 thus gives the aircraft a greatly enhanced capability in its anti-ship role, with an acceptable increase in weight.

The elements of the missile are shown in Figure 5.1 and its launching from a small ship is illustrated in Figure 5.2. The effect of the missile upon a minelayer is seen in Figure 5.3.

FIG. 5.2   Launching Penguin from a small ship. (*Kongsberg*)

Fɪɢ. 5.3   Damage to a minelayer by Penguin. (*Photo: Kongsberg*)

EXOCET

By far the best known anti-ship weapon is the French Exocet, made by the Aerospatiale company. Exocet is an antiship missile designed to be capable of disabling an enemy ship whose size justifies the use of such a weapon. Disabling a warship does not necessarily imply sinking it. An operational warship comprises a robust metal hull, containing propulsion machinery, fuel, electrical circuits, electronic systems, weapons, ammunition and explosives, and a crew. A 700 to 800 kg missile which penetrates the ship at over Mach 0.9 (1100 kph) and whose 160 kg warhead, in addition to its direct effect, acts on the ship's components like a huge detonator, will cause considerable damage: a breached hull, internal explosions; fires and toxic vapours; short circuits and, naturally, fragile electronics will be put out of action. Such effects, which occurred in the Falklands conflict, make arguments as to whether a warhead actually explodes or not purely academic.

A practice firing against a hull which has been emptied of all sensitive components (a disused ship) will produce a large hole but may not necessarily sink it. To be certain of sinking such a target, the warhead would need to be substantially increased, implying a missile of the Soviet SSN.3 type which has a warhead weighing about 1 metric ton and a gross weight of 4.7 tons. Such a design, obsolete in any case, results in a veritable monster that can be used only on very large ships and which has none of the qualities of accuracy, stealth and defence penetration capability that make Exocet what it is. In fact such a missile can be no more compared to Exocet than a Flying Fortress to a modern tactical support plane.

Logic has led first to the ultimate purpose of the weapon, i.e. the desired military result. The next requirement is for the missile to reach its destination, from which a certain number of imperatives derive:

Target detection by the launch platform, identification and designation to the missile's computer.

Accurate navigation.

The ability to penetrate the enemy defences.

Easy and dependable deployment.

The possibility for the launcher to escape enemy fire before and even after the missile is fired.

And by no means least, an important characteristic possessed by the missile: its small size, enabling it to be used by small vessels, planes or even helicopters.

These operational criteria have resulted in certain technical characteristics of the missile.

All-weather, fire-and-forget;

Solid fuel;

High speed in excess of Mach 0.9;

A range of 40 to 70 km, depending on the type of missile and launching conditions;

Inertial cruise navigation followed by target search and terminal homing using an active radar seeker;

Sea-skimming flight.

These criteria and the corresponding characteristics are of course difficult to analyse separately due to their many interactions. However, they endow Exocet with a remarkable overall coherence—which is the basis of its operational success.

One essential characteristic in the view of Aerospatiale is the choice of solid propellant because it provides that vital quality—reliability. This technology has been fully mastered: out of more than 200 Exocet test and combat firings, there has never been the slightest hitch where propulsion is concerned. The solid motors permit storage in sealed launcher canisters and avoid the drawbacks of jet-engine propulsion which are inherent in the need to store kerosene with the unavoidable risk of leaks; less dependable engine startup and attendant delays, and a more obtrusive radar signature, because the cross-section is larger and the shape of the engine's air intake amplifies the radar returns.

All the jet engine can offer to offset these serious drawbacks is great range. But from the operational viewpoint, even this advantage is somewhat illusory when the accuracy and stealth aspects are also considered.

The initially specified range—40 km for the MM 38—corresponds to the radar horizon of a medium-sized vessel (range is governed by the height of the antennas and the earth's curvature) and therefore permits launches based on the ship's detection means alone, ensuring full autonomy. In addition, the missile's flight time (about two minutes) does not allow the enemy vessel to move very far. Thus the search area will be small, enabling the missile's seeker to lock onto the target unambiguously in a few tenths of a second. Greater range requires an over-the-horizon target designation to be performed by a vector other than the launching ship.

This is the case with the MM 40 which has a range of 70 km and uses a relay helicopter that climbs to a sufficient altitude to permit target search and designation, then descends immediately for maximum stealth. For much greater ranges, there are two possible solutions: using the airborne relay to update the missile along its trajectory (requiring it to remain in radar contact with the target throughout the first part of the flight and to transmit radio commands, thus negating any claim to stealth): or else the missile is left to its own devices, in which case the target's movements and the imprecision resulting from lengthy inertial navigation would mean a large search area for the seeker head. But notwithstanding the advances made in seeker technology, the risk of target confusion remains, together with the need for tighter manoeuvres. Thus, for a given speed, a significant increase in range entails uncertainty about the outcome. In the case of the air-launched AM 39, which has a range of 50–70 km depending on launching conditions, the rapidity of the launch platform and its ability to turn back at very low altitude immediately after firing make an extended range capability useless for all practical purposes. In the Falklands campaign, none of the Argentinian Étendard aircraft were hit or even seem to have been threatened at the time of the Exocet launchings. Lethal and accurate though it may be, the missile must still be able to pass through the enemy defences. In other words, it must possess 'penetration capability'.

Various factors contribute to this:

> Sea skimming flight, at increasingly lower levels as the target is approached that can be programmed according to the sea state.
> High speed in excess of Mach 0.9.
> Inertial navigation for total stealth up to proximity of the search area.
> A high-performance seeker ensuring very rapid locking onto the target.
> Thanks to its ability to discriminate, the seeker is claimed to be virtually immune to electronic countermeasures, such as decoys or chaff.
> A small radar signature.
> A low peaking altitude at launch (about 30 m) (less than that of a turbojet powered missile), ensuring an unobtrusive launch.
> Salvo firings in the case of the MM 40 (at least four missiles in 10 seconds), causing saturation of the defences.

Of course, an Exocet is not completely invulnerable and a Seawolf surface-to-air defensive missile has been able to score a hit under test-range conditions.

Chaff is claimed to become almost totally ineffective once a seeker has locked onto its target, the more so as Exocet, from the outset of its design, has benefited from all the advances made in homing-head technology, especially in the field of electronic counter-countermeasures. The rapid-firing guns of the Phalanx or Goalkeeper type, constitute the ultimate defence because of their short range. When it is remembered that a direct hit—and that on the warhead itself—is required to neutralize an Exocet, it seems to Aerospatiale that its penetration chances may hardly be affected. So far no systematic tests have been conducted against a missile in flight by CIWS guns and their effectiveness against Exocet is not established, according to Aerospatiale. In any case, the defences would stand a smaller chance against several missiles succeeding one another at two-second intervals. The other significant advantage possessed by this solid-propellant missile is its ease of deployment from a wide variety

Fig. 5.4   Exocet firing from a ship. (*Photo: Aerospatiale*)

of launch platforms. The fact that it is packaged in launcher canisters of minimum
bulk enables it to be installed on small-tonnage vessels while at the same time
reducing maintenance to a few automatically run tests. As for the air-launched
version, it can be fired from combat or maritime patrol planes, or from helicopters;
in fact Exocet is currently probably the only missile in its class in operational service
on helicopters (the Super Frelon and Super Puma). Meanwhile, the SM39 version,
now in service with the French Navy, is capable of being deployed in conventional or
nuclear submarines and launched from standard torpedo-tubes.

The basic design is incorporated in a family of three missiles which have been in
operational service since 1972 and have been adopted for different launching
platforms. All the variants have the common characteristics mentioned above of:

> Fire-and-forget missile.
> All weather firing capability.
> Inertial navigation followed by active radar automatic guidance.
> Sea skimming flight altitude (variable according to sea state).
> Solid propellant in two stages (boost and sustain).

Speed: Mach 0.93.

Range of 40–70 km depending on missile type and firing conditions.

The constant improvement of missile components, particularly guidance equipment, using the latest technology.

Exocets are extremely difficult to detect and decoy. A salvo firing capability also provides the possibility of saturating enemy defences. These two development lines enable Exocet to keep its lead over competing missiles and over current defence systems.

Exocet, in all its variants, has proved its great operational effectiveness in combat.

MM38: is a surface-to-surface missile, capable of destroying all types of surface vessel. Its 42 km range is in line with the range of the launcher vessel's own sensors. Equipping 18 navies, including the major European forces, it has been fitted on 180 vessels of all types. The in-service missile reliability rate is 94 percent. A direct hit percentage of the same order has been recorded after a large number of operational firings.

AM39 is an air-to-surface version of the Exocet family, which has all the same features and qualities, notably the fire and forget guidance and sea-skimming flight path. It has a range of 50 to 70 kms, depending on the altitude and speed of the launcher aircraft, which can thus go into attack from beyond the range of surface air defence systems. It has been in service since 1978 in the French and several other navies and has been installed on helicopters (particularly the Super-Frelon and Super-Puma) and strike fighters (Super-Étendard, Mirage 50 and Mirage F1) and maritime patrol aircraft (Atlantic Nouvelle Generation).

MM40 is a surface-to-surface missile derived from the MM38, benefiting from improvements in a number of respects. It has a greater power of penetration of enemy defences and a capability for salvo firing with some missiles kept in reserve. It uses a cylindrical, small-diameter container-launcher and it employs an over-the-horizon firing capability using target designation by a relay helicopter, with the guidance remaining of the fire and forget type. The 70 km range is optimal for a high subsonic, fire and forget missile. The MM40, now in mass production, has been purchased by the French Navy and some ten other countries. It is also available in a coastal battery version.

SM39 is submarine-launched. It is housed in a powered and guided underwater capsule, and is launched from a standard torpedo tube.

The Exocet missile is 5.21 m in length and weighs 735 kg, so it is a large and heavy projectile which, even without the damage caused by the exploding warhead, can cause great structural devastation in a frigate when it hits at a velocity of Mach 1. The missile steering is by aerodynamic control surfaces and constant up-dating of its guidance and homing methods now make the latest versions even more difficult to decoy. The MM40 salvo firing capability gives a possibility of saturating the defence, which adds markedly to its effectiveness.

The next generation of Exocets, known as ANS, will be supersonic with a speed of Mach 2, a range of up to 200 km, ramjet propulsion and a very high defence penetration power. They are expected to enter service by 1994 and will include all the

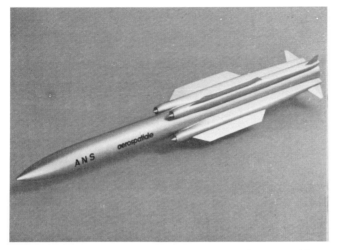

FIG. 5.5   The next generation of Exocet—ANS. (*Aerospatiale*)

versions of the current Exocets. An Exocet firing from a ship is shown in Figure 5.4 and the new ANS missile is seen in Figure 5.5.

SEA EAGLE

The British anti-ship missiles produced by British Aerospace are sophisticated second generation developments which can be fired from ships or aircraft. The larger missile is Sea Eagle which weighs some 600 kg and is just over 4 m long.

In its design, particular attention has been given to the radar and EW aspects of its performance and in consequence it is said to be very effective in reaching its target without being decoyed.

Modern warships are equipped with radars and sensing devices which can detect and warn of approaching missiles so that countermeasures and decoys can be deployed. To counter early warning, Sea Eagle can be launched outside the range of the warship's radar, and will descend to a sea skimming height where it will be below the warship's radar horizon and among the sea clutter. Even if the launch aircraft is detected during the pre-launch phase, the target ship has no confirmation that an attack has been launched, or, if it has, from which direction the missile will approach. Particular attention has been paid to suppressing stray radiation from the missile's systems which might reveal its presence.

Once launched, the missile navigates using information given to its onboard computer prior to release. The radar seeker remains silent until it comes within radar range of the target; the radar seeker is then switched on and acquires the target. Lock-on is rapid and takes place at extended range because of the high power of the Sea Eagle seeker and the special features of its search technique. Even in the presence of jamming, the missile seeker's high power will burn through and lock-on at an early stage. The target ship is therefore denied the opportunity of detecting the missile easily and deploying its electronic defences before missile lock-on occurs.

Thus the effectiveness of the countermeasures subsequently deployed is considerably reduced.

Thereafter the target is unlikely to break lock because of the missile's ECCM suite which the seeker's computer can use to defeat enemy countermeasures. Sea Eagle is therefore expected to win the radar battle, which is the vital precursor to a successful attack, and emerge successfully to eradicate the ship threat. Sea Eagle is propelled by a turbojet engine which gives the missile a high subsonic cruising speed in all weathers. The engine, which has a low infra-red signature and is smoke-free, is a Microturbo type TRI-60 having a three-stage axial flow compressor, a straight through annular combustion chamber and a single stage turbine. The simple design has been extensively tested and has proved highly reliable.

The Sea Eagle active radar seeker is designed and manufactured by Marconi Defence Systems and is a high power, pulse radar which is capable of detecting targets at extended ranges. This advanced seeker can respond very effectively to defeat countermeasures which might be employed to deceive or to decoy the missile away from its intended target.

It has a re-programmable computer which acts as a central brain, controlling the detection, acquisition and tracking of a desired target from a group of less valued targets.

The Sea Eagle warhead is a disabling system designed to penetrate a warship's outer structure and to explode within the vessel, causing maximum damage to its fighting systems. Even the largest vessels, with multiple systems and sophisticated damage control arrangements, are likely to suffer crippling damage from Sea Eagle strikes.

The missile's sea skimming trajectory ensures that the warhead will impact and penetrate the target at a height above the waterline calculated to cause maximum damage. The effect of the large warhead is augmented by the ignition of residual fuel and the kinetic energy of the missile structure. The design of the warhead ensures penetration of ship structures even at glancing angles.

The destructive capability of Sea Eagle has been demonstrated in fully guided tests against targets at sea. A missile was launched from a Sea Harrier at low altitude and flew a pre-programmed sea-skimming course before hitting the target ship, the former guided missile destroyer, HMS *Devonshire*, 6800 tons. The missile scored a direct hit, causing extensive damage to the ship which, in operational circumstances, would have resulted in complete disablement.

Sea Eagle has been designed as a round of ammunition, it can be taken from store and installed on an aircraft without testing or preparation. Loading on to the aircraft is quick and straightforward. Selection of the missile and firing is simple and quick. Before launch the missile is supplied with information on the target position and other data to enable it to navigate to the target. This information is normally supplied from the launch aircraft's navigation/attack system automatically, but it can be relayed to the launch aircraft from other sources and entered manually. When grouped targets are encountered, the aircrew can also program the missile with target selection criteria.

Sea Eagle can be launched at heights ranging from very low level to high altitude. Large offset angles can be accommodated by the system. After launch, the missile is autonomous. The turbojet engine ignites as the missile descends to sea skimming height. The missile navigates towards the target under the control of its onboard computer, using the information supplied to it before launch. When appropriate, the target seeker is switched on and searches for the target. Lock-on is rapidly achieved after which the target seeker guides the missile to target impact. At the start of the terminal phase of flight, the missile lowers its sea skimming height to ensure an impact close to the waterline.

As there is no interference between missiles, they can be fired in ripple sequence from aircraft. Missiles in ripple sequence can be directed at different targets or, if thought necessary, at the same target.

In the absence of accurate target information or if target information cannot be supplied to it, the missile can be launched on the expected target bearing and will still have a high probability of intercepting and destroying it.

Sea Eagle SL is the ship-launched version designed to provide ships down to 200 tons with an over-the-horizon strike capability against hostile warships.

FIG. 5.6   Ship-Launched Sea Eagle. (*Photo: Marconi Defence Systems*)

The missile is housed in a sealed box which protects it during transport and acts as a launcher when mounted on a ship's deck. Two solid propellant boosters accelerate the missile to its operational flight speed when the air-breathing gas turbine takes over and the spent boosters are jettisoned.

Sea Eagle SL accepts target data supplied from the ship's Action Information Organisation (AIO). This data may have been obtained by the ship's own surveillance radars, or have been relayed over a data link from helicopters, aircraft or other ships and relate to targets beyond the ship's horizon. It can be launched on a heading totally different from the target bearing. Following launch, the missile will steer itself onto the correct interception course. Launch of the missiles is controlled from the Sea Eagle SL weapon console in the ship's operations room.

In its box launcher, the missile requires no pre-flight testing or maintenance on board ship. Box launchers can be assembled in groups of one to six on mountings provided at suitable locations on a ship's deck. The same launcher mountings as Lightweight Sea Dart can be used for it so that light naval craft can be armed with a mix of both weapons appropriate to the particular missions on which they are engaged.

Sea Eagle SL could also be used in the coastal defence role fired from land-based launchers.

The firing of a ship-launched Sea Eagle, with external boosters is shown in Figure 5.6.

SEA SKUA

This British Aerospace missile is a smaller and lighter sea-skimmer than Sea Eagle and is intended for fitting to small ships, helicopters and light aircraft. It uses a semi-active radar homer and thus a number can be fired in ripple formation to saturate defences. The missile is 2.5 m long and weighs 145 kg and has an all weather capability. It is in service with the Royal Navy and has been selected by three other navies.

As a lightweight weapon system, Sea Skua can be fitted to small shipborne helicopters. Such helicopters with their radars and other sensor systems are important in providing their parent ship with early warning of the presence of hostile ships, particularly in waters where fast attack craft armed with ship-to-ship missiles are operating. With Sea Skua installed, the reconnaissance helicopter can also attack these hostile vessels before they can approach close enough to launch their ship-to-ship missiles. The helicopter's parent ship may remain passive and undetected and is able to conserve its main armament for use against other higher value targets.

Sea Skua can also be fitted to a wide range of other helicopters and fixed wing aircraft operating in various other roles from both ship and land bases.

In a typical engagement, after search for, detection and identification of the target, the helicopter closes at low level to a suitable attack position. Here it climbs to missile release height, the aircrew select a missile and set its terminal sea skimming height on the Control Indicator Group. This panel indicates when the missile is armed and ready for launch. The helicopter's radar points at and illuminates the ship target and the missile's homing head locks on to the reflections from the target. After release, the missile drops for a short distance under autopilot control until the rocket motor ignites. During the boost phase, the azimuth and height guidance loops are closed. The missile then descends to an intermediate sea skimming height under radio altimeter control for a short period before descending to the terminal sea skimming height selected before launch. The homing head guides the missile in azimuth to impact with the target. The single shot hit probability is very high. The warhead is exploded after penetrating the ship's structure and has a high degree of lethality.

The launch helicopter is not prohibited from manoeuvring after the missile has been released, except within the general limits required to maintain illumination of the target by the helicopter's radar. If the radar has a 360 degree scan capability the launch helicopter can turn completely away from the target.

Sea Skua is a disabling weapon system intended to destroy the weapon control systems of the smaller warships. A single Sea Skua missile has a very high probability of achieving this object when fired against corvettes of up to 1000 tons, fast patrol boats, assault craft, hydrofoils and hovercraft. The missile's range is in excess of 15 km, which allows the launch aircraft to stay out of reach of the target ship's point defence systems.

Sea Skua missiles can also be fired in rapid succession; this adds to its effectiveness when used against destroyer sized targets. Trials have demonstrated the capability of the warhead to penetrate steel plating of the thickness expected in this type of ship. The advantages of better damage control and duplication of systems enjoyed by larger vessels are offset by the ability of Sea Skua missiles to be fired in ripple sequence in co-ordinated attacks from two or more aircraft launch platforms.

Sea Skua is approximately one third of the weight and costs significantly less than the larger anti-ship missiles. It therefore represents a highly cost-effective solution to the major threat posed by small vessels armed with long range anti-ship missiles which are now being operated in increasing numbers by many navies.

Sea Skua has been designed to operate successfully in the testing conditions and environments it can expect to meet in service life around the globe. It was used with outstanding success in combat in the South Atlantic in 1982 when all missiles fired found their targets, despite the need to operate in the most severe weather conditions. Equipment returned afterwards from the battle area was also found to be fully serviceable. The high standards of reliability achieved are the result of a comprehensive development programme and British Aerospace's stringent quality control procedures during all stages of manufacture and test.

Sea Skua is delivered, stored and handled in a trolley which permits the missile to be simply and quickly loaded directly on to the helicopter using a standard ammunition hoist. The wings and fins are stowed in pockets on the side of the trolley and are fitted to the missile after it has been loaded. The system has been designed for rapid role change. Helicopters can be fitted with common weapon carriers, capable of carrying lightweight torpedoes or other weapons as an alternative to Sea Skua if desired. Therefore, a helicopter with a Sea Skua capability is a true multi-role aircraft. Like Sea Eagle, the Sea Skua missile has been designed and developed to be treated as a 'round of ammunition', no testing being necessary during operational deployment. The only inspection required at first line is a visual one for physical damage. Depending on the operational scenario, it is recommended that the missile be returned periodically to a depot facility for replacement of life-expired items, a functional test and subsequent return to ready-for-use storage.

FIG. 5.7   Sea Skua in flight. (*Photo: British Aerospace*)

The aircraft installed equipment is tested for correct functioning before operational use, using a portable test set. Should any failures occur, further testing takes place at the base workshop. Drill missiles are available for training purposes to familiarise maintenance crews with handling and loading procedures, and a simulator can be carried in the aircraft to provide training for the flight crew.

Sea Skua SL (ship launched) is a new version of the combat-proven sea-skimming anti-ship missile specifically developed as a low-cost lightweight weapon for installation on small naval boats and hovercraft. Fired from such craft operating in a coastal defence role, Sea Skua SL can strike targets out to horizon range. The small boat weapon uses the same standard Sea Skua missile and Ferranti Seaspray radar of the helicopter weapon system. A Sea Skua SL system is ideally suited for installation on boats down to 20 m (65 ft) in length.

A Sea Skua SL weapon system comprises a Ferranti Seaspray surveillance and illuminating radar, a one-man weapon control console and simple deck-mounted launchers. Fixed in elevation and azimuth, two twin-canister launchers, one angled to starboard the other to port, can be fitted on the rear deck of a light strike craft. The weapon control console occupies less than 0.5 cubic metres and is installed in the boat's command area. The compact lightweight Ferranti Seaspray radar is mounted on the ship's mast under a protective radome. Of robust construction, the radar is well able to cope with the masthead environment. With the radar antenna assembly weighing 30 kg, the weapon control console 140 kg and a twin canister launcher with missiles 692 kg, most of the system weight is concentrated at deck level.

To initiate an engagement, the weapon operator at the console selects the missile to be fired and, dependent upon the type of target and the current sea state, sets the terminal sea-skimming height for the missile. An indication is given at the console when the missile is armed and ready. The operator can then fire the missile. Following launch, the azimuth and height control circuits are activated, the missile's

FIG. 5.8   Artist's impression of Ship-Launched Sea Skua. (*British Aerospace*)

homing head locks-on to the radar reflections from the target and guides it in azimuth until impact. Following completion of the boost phase, the missile first descends to an intermediate height under the control of a radio altimeter, and then to the pre-selected sea-skimming height for the final approach. The installation of Sea Skua SL in small light craft provides a new economical and effective solution to the problem of coastal defence. The missile is seen in Fig. 5.7 and an artist's impression of its firing from a small craft is given in Fig. 5.8.

OTOMAT

The Italian company Oto Melara SPA produce a large and sophisticated sea skimming anti-ship missile called OTOMAT. This has a range of 60 km and a high single shot kill probability with a 210 kg warhead which includes more than 60 kg of explosive. This missile has a proximity fuse as well as an impact fuse so that, if it overflies a small target, the warhead will be detonated. Its propulsion is by means of a turbo-jet engine.

Otomat is a naval surface-to-surface missile system suitable for installation in ships of any tonnage, including patrol craft. The system can be employed against enemy ships irrespective of their relative bearing, without varying own ship's course. It operates in adverse weather conditions with sea states up to Force 7. This capability allows immediate attack on the enemy, as soon as it is detected.

The main components of the system are a control console, a computer, the launchers (from two to eight according to type of installation) and the missiles.

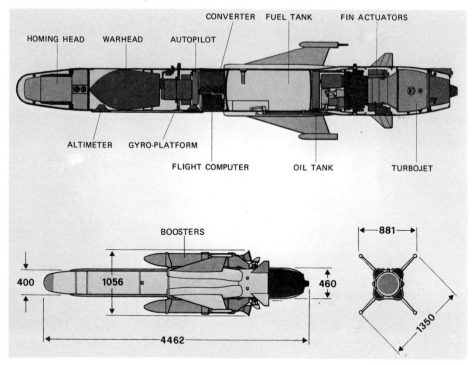

FIG. 5.9   Construction of the Otomat Missile. (*Oto Melara*)

The ship's search radar is used to acquire the target. The target data, obtained by active and passive ship's sensors, are processed by the Otomat System which supplies the missile with all information relating to flight and target prior to launching. The system can use information supplied through data links from other ships, aircraft or helicopters, for launch and missile guidance.

Long endurance allows the missile to cover any likely detection range, even extending beyond the radar horizon. During flight, the guidance mode is inertial, preventing enemy detection of the launch or missile approach. The radar seeker comes into operation near the target. Reaction time for the enemy is consequently extremely brief, and does not allow much time for evasive action or effective defence. Destructive capability is such as to sink small ships, heavily damage medium tonnage ships, and incapacitate larger vessels.

Since the missile endurance is so great and the operational capability so flexible, the Otomat System possesses significant development potential, so that it is likely to remain a highly effective system for at least ten years.

Otomat Missile launching includes: 'preparation for launch', which involves the whole system, and 'missile flight', when the missile is independent from the launching system.

All launching operations are started and monitored by the Otomat console operator. Preparation for launch includes start of the turbo-jet, and activation of all the electronic equipment of the missile. During this phase, all guidance data are

FIG. 5.10   Flight profile of Otomat. The missile is shown being fired from a frigate. (*Oto Melara*)

supplied to the missile by the launching computer. This phase, which ends when the missile leaves the ship, can be aborted at any moment before booster ignition.

The missile flight comprises the launching phase, the cruising phase and the attack phase. The launching phase starts with the booster ignition and ends when the boosters separate from the missile. During this phase, the missile reaches its cruising speed. Following the booster separation, the missile descends to a constant cruising height and assumes the interception course.

In the cruising phase, the missile, controlled by its pseudo inertial guidance system, approaches the target following a sea skimming height profile. Pseudo inertial flight is regulated automatically by equipment contained on board the missile on the basis of data memorized prior to launch.

The attack phase includes the target search and the descent to the impact height. Target search begins when the radar seeker comes into operation. After lock on, the homing head guides the missile onto the target, using proportional navigation. Both search height and impact height depend on the sea state which is calculated by the missile itself during the approach phase. Since the operational period of the seeker is extremely short and the missile attack height in this phase is very low, the chances of detection and destruction by the enemy are minimal. Missile flight terminates on hitting the target. The destructive effect is increased since the effect of the combustion of the remaining missile fuel load is added to the warhead charge. If the missile overflies a small target, the warhead will be exploded by the proximity fuse with which the missile is also fitted.

The speed of the missile is M0.9 and the warhead is capable of piercing up to 90 mm of armoured plate at an angle of impact of 90 degrees. Otomat is scheduled for installation in 62 ships ranging from a helicopter carrier to a small hydrofoil and including frigates, corvettes and fast patrol boats. The missile construction is shown in Figure 5.9 and its flight profile is illustrated in Figure 5.10.

A SMALL ANTI-SHIP MISSILE FOR SUBMARINES—SLAM

While submerged submarines can launch large anti-ship missiles such as Exocet and Harpoon these are expensive devices which are only appropriate for high-value surface targets. Of interest is a quite different missile designed for firing from surfaced submarines and small surface craft against lesser ship and helicopter targets at close range. It is known as SLAM and it gives a useful surface attack capability to conventional (non-nuclear) submarines in particular, over a range of a few kilometres under conditions of adequate visibility.

SLAM was originally designed to match submarines which undertake roles in which a surface attack capability would be valuable. It enables the submarine to attack shallow-draft craft, such as fast patrol boats, as well as hovercraft and helicopters. Selective punishment may also be inflicted on merchant ships.

A surface version of SLAM is also under development for hovercraft fast patrol boats, and other coastal craft whose armament is limited. The prototype system is currently undergoing trials, first on a land vehicle, then at sea. The launcher assembly carries six Blowpipe missiles clustered around a central electronics enclosure which contains part of the missile control equipment, television camera and gyro sub-system for launcher stabilisation. The missiles and their associated canisters form part of the standard Blowpipe system.

SLAM can be fitted in new construction submarines or retrospectively, without major re-working. A rapid fit version is also available to meet particular operational needs. Fitting on surface craft will be possible without significant modification in most cases.

Submarine control-room equipment consists of an operator display panel, power supplies and control units for the television and launcher servo-control systems. Built-in test facilities are provided to enable routine servicing and rapid system checks to be carried out without the need for specialist personnel. Provision can be made for storing re-loads, their quantity and location depending on customer requirements.

Target acquisition is accomplished by means of the search periscope, or an optical sight on surface craft, the launcher being automatically aligned with the target in azimuth. The operator locates the target by means of a controller and elevation indicator and takes entire control of the launcher, using a two-motion velocity controller, freeing the periscope or optical sight for general surveillance. After firing, the missile is tracked visually through the television system on to the target, using the same two-motion controller.

SLAM is being developed by Vickers to meet the need on submarines and light surface craft for an effective close-range armament against other surface vessels and helicopters. The system uses the Blowpipe missile, currently being produced by Short Brothers.

6

Point Defence Missiles

Point defence missiles are employed to defend only the ship upon which they are fitted. They are relatively short range devices and have gained enormous potential importance as one of, if not the most important of, the elements of defence against sea-skimming anti-ship missiles. In the concept of layered defence, the aim of the two outer layers would be the destruction of the missile firing platform by aircraft or long range missiles, the middle or third layer would consist of point defence missiles and the inner or fourth layer of the fast firing gun as a CIWS (Close in Weapon System) and electronic warfare decoys. The aim of the outer layer may be difficult to achieve, as the missile firing platform will probably be difficult to detect before it fires. The inner layer provides the 'last ditch' defence of each individual vessel. Thus the PDMS (Point Defence Missile System) is accorded absolutely prime importance in the eyes of many tactical experts. Because the very short warning time of missile attack (typically 25 seconds) does not enable men to take the necessary decisions and then to initiate appropriate action, it is virtually essential that the PDMS should be automatic in operation. This requirement places a very high demand on the quality of the system's software if it is to be both effective and adequately proof against false alarms in its target selection.

Of course, point defence missile systems also have a role against attacking aircraft. They vary in sophistication, cost and performance from manually controlled missiles, such as the Short Brothers SEACAT, which is widely fitted and used as a relatively simple system, mainly against aircraft, to the fully automatic SEAWOLF made by British Aerospace which was the first anti-missile missile system in the West designed as such from its inception and now well combat-proven in the Falklands War.

SEAWOLF

The missile is 2 m in length and weighs 80 kg; it is handled on board ship as a round of ammunition and requires no maintenance or testing. The Seawolf system is all-weather and very rapid in operation covering an engagement zone from low level to high elevation out to a range of several kilometres. The propulsion is by means of a solid fuel rocket motor which accelerates the missile to a supersonic speed beyond Mach 2. After this has burnt out, the missile coasts to its target. The warhead is a blast type, detonated by impact or a proximity fuse. The guidance and control are by command of a radar or television (for low level targets) line-of-sight; fixed uniform wings are mounted on the central part of the body and control finds at the rear are operated by a gas generator.

Target acquisition, missile launch and the flight to target are initiated and controlled entirely automatically unless prevented by manual intervention. The detection and evaluation of threats is a complex procedure also performed automatically (following target evaluation and weapon assignment rules (TEWA)) by the weapon system control computers on board ship. To reduce the cost per round to a minimum, and to maximise reliability, all missile guidance computations are also performed on board ship resulting in the minimum of electronic equipment being carried in the missiles.

Two Royal Navy Type 22 frigates armed with Seawolf served in the Falklands campaign—HMS Broadsword and HMS Brilliant. These two ships were credited with destroying five hostile aircraft. In one engagement two aircraft in an attacking formation of four were shot down by Seawolf missiles, the third crashed into the sea while taking evasive action. Only the fourth, and sole survivor, of the group escaped. No opportunity occurred during the campaign for Seawolf to engage anti-ship missiles. In a representative operational trial conducted later by the Royal Navy, a Seawolf missile successfully intercepted and destroyed an Exocet sea-skimming anti-ship missile. The effectiveness of Seawolf has been demonstrated on numerous occasions, successfully intercepting small supersonic rocket targets and 4.5 calibre shells fired from naval guns.

The Seawolf GWS25 weapon system utilizes a six-barrel launcher, trainable in azimuth and elevation. Targets are detected and identified as hostile by the ship's surveillance radars. The threat is evaluated and the target to be engaged is allocated to the Seawolf tracker radar associated with a particular missile launcher. Both tracker and launcher slew round to face the approaching threat and the tracker searches in elevation until the target is acquired. The tracker locks-on establishing a radar line of sight to the target. When within range, a Seawolf missile is automatically launched and gathered into the tracking beam. The position of the missile relative to the centre of the tracking beam is detected by the radar and the weapon system guidance computer on board ship generates the necessary steering commands to bring the missile into the centre of the beam and keep it flying up the beam until interception. Steering commands are relayed to the missile over a microwave link. The tracker operates in I band and the command links in J band. Two independently-controlled missiles can be fired at the same target.

The Seawolf GWS25 weapon system is in operational service aboard the Royal Navy's Type 22 frigates. Five Royal Navy Leander-class frigates have also been renovated with the system.

New variants of the weapon are now being developed. The GWS26 (vertical launch) VL Seawolf system is being built and the Royal Navy's Type 23 frigates will be the first class of ship to be equipped with this high performance weapon. Vertical launch VL Seawolf is a lightweight system that uses the same basic Seawolf missile with the addition of a tandem booster motor. In essence, VL Seawolf is a new weapon that possesses significant operational advantages over the earlier Seawolf systems. Vertical launching virtually eliminates blind arcs of fire from a ship, increases the effective interception range of Seawolf and enables the weapon to defeat saturation attacks. It is a rapid-reaction weapon. Versatile ship installations are possible as the vertical launch canisters can be located singly, in clusters, or in silos, above or below decks to suit the particular design of ship. Launcher maintenance is eliminated.

A VL Seawolf missile is stored and transported in its canister from which it is fired.

FIG. 6.1   Seawolf firing from a ship of the Royal Navy. (*Photo: British Aerospace*)

The canister has a frangible cover and integral vertical exhaust ducting. The vertical launch concept was proven as long ago as 1968 when seven Seawolf-type missiles were successfully fired and 'turned over' in flight. Immediately following launch, when clear of the ship's superstructure, the Seawolf missile and booster assembly performs a turnover manoeuvre onto the heading of the approaching target, after which the booster is discarded. The missile is then gathered into the beam of the tracker radar and the remainder of the Seawolf interception sequence is performed in the usual manner. VL Seawolf is equipped with an inertial measuring unit which provides the necessary attitude and motion data needed to enable the turnover manoeuvre to be performed rapidly, with great precision. The boost motor has thrust vector control.

A series of vertical launch trials with VL Seawolf missiles have been completed successfully. The trials were conducted at sea from Longbow, a 12,000 tonne barge specially equipped with launchers and all the necessary support facilities to serve as a self-contained trials platform. These trials are described in Chapter 3.

A more advanced GWS27 Seawolf system to counter the threat posed by the more capable anti-ship missiles that will be entering service in the next century is under development. Various new units have been designed for use in Seawolf weapon systems of lower all-up weight, suitable for installation on smaller ships down to 400 tonnes displacement. Two new lightweight tracker radars of improved performance have been produced. One is the VM40 radar built by Hollandse Signaalapparaten and the other is the Type 911 built by Marconi.

A new tracker radar was required for Seawolf to counter the threat posed to naval vessels by sea-skimming anti-ship missiles. The problem is that at low radar angles, multipath returns and interference from the sea surface reduce tracking accuracy when low level targets such as sea-skimming missiles are to be engaged. The solution is to use a dual-frequency pulse doppler tracker radar which eliminates these effects. Both the Signaal VM40 and the Type 911 radars are of this type. The feasibility of the concept has been proved during trials of the Signaal VM40 radar and the associated fire control system which successfully demonstrated its ability to direct standard Seawolf missiles to intercept missile size targets at all heights down to sea level, and also its ability accurately to track at adequate ranges, manoeuvring aircraft and low-flying sea-skimming targets against land and sea clutter.

The British Government has selected the Type 911 radar for all the Royal Navy's new-built Seawolf ships. The 1802SW is another lightweight guidance system for Seawolf proposed by Marconi. It is a hybrid system utilising radar to track the target, and a thermal imaging system to track the missile. A lightweight four-missile launcher for Seawolf has been built and proved in firing trials.

A Seawolf firing from the six missile launcher on board a Royal Navy ship is shown in Figure 6.1.

ALBATROS

The Albatros point defence missile system uses the Aspide or Sea Sparrow missiles and an eight-compartment launcher provided by Oto Melara which can be installed on warships ranging in size from corvettes upwards. The launcher, without missiles has a weight of 6.5 tons; it can elevate from −5 to +80 degrees at a speed of 25 degrees per second and in azimuth it can be trained at 45 degrees per second. This PDMS is typical of the fast reaction now required for the defence of ships against low flying aircraft and missiles and it provides an important defensive strength for modern warships.

SEASTREAK AND SEACAT

At the other end of the scale of sophistication and cost are two important and effective point defence systems made by Shorts where design and modern technology have been used to provide very low cost systems which have an effective performance. The prime design objective of low cost is very important for the future of naval surface weapons and is as great a challenge as the achievement of very high performance at a much greater cost. These missiles are therefore of special significance. Seastreak is particularly interesting as it can be seen as a hybrid between a missile and a precision guided projectile, and it competes against the fast firing guns of CIWS which are, in general, considerably more expensive.

Short Brothers of Belfast entered the guided weapons arena some thirty five years ago developing actuators for the control of surface to air test vehicles. This work resulted in the Seacat missile system. Replacing the 40 mm Bofors gun, it was the first point defence guided missile system in operation on vessels of the Royal Navy. Since

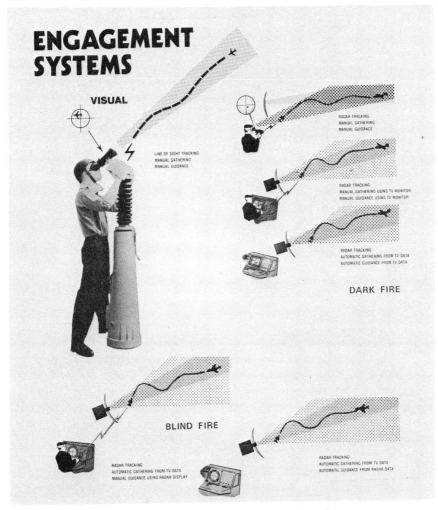

Fig. 6.2   Seacat engagement systems. (*Shorts*)

entering service in 1962, the Seacat system has been sold to fifteen navies overseas. The main reason for its success rests in the simplicity of the system. While subsequent systems for air defence tended to follow the trend towards complexity and autonomy, Shorts' philosophy was to produce a simple manual system capable of fulfilling the assigned task. This resulted in a *low cost* system with maximum reliability.

The Seacat missile is a small sub-sonic unit with a large high-explosive blast warhead and proximity fuse. The motor comprises two stages—boost and sustain, and its manoeuvrability is superior to that of any known low-level supersonic attack aircraft. Range is in excess of five kilometres. No pre-firing 'warm-up' sequences are required and auxiliary power services within the missile are activated at launch.

Over the years, by a series of controlled steps, Seacat has been continually upgraded as operational experience has accumulated. As a result, it has now been integrated with a large variety of tracking radars and television systems to provide a

Fɪɢ. 6.3   Seacat firing from a multiple shipboard launcher. (*Photo: Shorts*)

fully automatic dark fire and full blind fire capability, enabling it to be operated in all weathers. In addition, a height control facility has been incorporated which allows the missile to be flown at programmed sea-skimming levels against surface targets or shore based installations without danger of ditching. This facility is incorporated in one of the missile's four control surfaces and can be readily introduced by customers into existing missile stocks. While these developments have been incorporated, the basic principle of retaining the option of manual operation has never been compromised. This aspect was found most beneficial in 1982 when Royal Navy vessels were operating in the confined waters of the Falklands where the radars were limited in their operation.

The Seacat system's compact, weight-saving design is emphasised in the Lightweight Seacat System which can be fitted, or retro-fitted, on vessels down to fast patrol boat size. Five principal units are involved, the pedestal director, from which the missile is fired and guided; the control officer's panel and the missile launch platform, all of which are deck mounted. Below decks are the guidance transmitter and the launcher control unit. The all up weight of the system is approximately 2 tonnes of which 15 per cent is distributed below decks.

Operation of the basic system is by the control officer and aimer receiving 'aircraft alarm' over the intercom system. The aimer at the pedestal director, acting on target bearing information received via the intercom, acquires the target in his binoculars and presses the 'Target Acquired' switch at his right handgrip. The control officer selects the appropriate missile on the launcher resulting in the 'System Ready'

Fig. 6.4   General appearance of Seastreak and its three darts. (*Photo: Shorts*)

indication on the control officer's panel showing green. 'Open Fire' is ordered, thereby switching the 'Open Fire' indication on the control officer's panel to red. The control officer sets the Intercept Switch to 'Fire' and verbally instructs the aimer, via the intercomm, to fire. The aimer presses the firing trigger at his right hand causing the two stage motors and the flares to ignite. The aimer acquires the missile in his binoculars and guides it via his thumb joystick into coincidence with the target until impact. After the engagement is complete and before the next firing, the transmitter is returned to the 'ready' state in preparation for the next engagement.

The basic concept of a simple, cheap missile controlled by a thumb-operated joystick, through a radio command link has been retained in the design of the man portable systems, Blowpipe and its successor, Javelin. While the basic mode of operation of these systems is firing from the shoulder, their effectiveness can be enhanced by operation from a 3-round multiple launcher. Using Javelin, with Semi Automatic Command to Line of Sight (SACLOS) guidance via a radio link, the in-built stabilisation in the Javelin aiming unit enhances its capability on the multiple launcher on board naval vessels. While the system is not applicable to small patrol craft it does provide very effective defence on board other naval craft and in particular the RFA's (Royal Fleet Auxiliaries) and STUFT (ships taken up from trade) in time of conflict. Since the system is lightweight and self-contained with no external power supplies, ship fitting is reduced to a minimum. The Royal Marines, who effectively deployed the Blowpipe system on board ship during the Falklands conflict, now deploy Javelin in the shoulder launcher mode. Currently, an evaluation of the multiple launcher is being undertaken to determine its applicability on board certain vessels where protection of merchant shipping may be desirous, if not essential.

Javelin consists of a missile, sealed in a canister, which acts as a launcher, and the aiming unit which consists of a stabilised tracking system and an auto guidance system. In general terms, the operator, using the stabilised tracking system, tracks the target throughout the engagement. A miniature television camera, aligned with the operator's stabilised sight-line, detects the missile by means of its flares and computes automatically the necessary guidance demands to bring and maintain the missile on the sight-line, the signals being conveyed by a radio link to the missile. The system also includes compensations for crosswinds and low-level targets and automatically generates a lead-angle to launch the missile ahead of crossing targets.

The concept of SACLOS guidance has been retained for the next generation of missile systems from Shorts. Starstreak, initially conceived as a private venture by the company in the late 1970s was chosen by the Ministry of Defence in late 1986 when a contract was placed for the development and initial production of Starstreak for the British Army. The basic system will initially be deployed in the early 1990s on board the Alvis Stormer armoured vehicle, with a lightweight multiple launcher and shoulder launched equipment contained within the vehicle for use in reversionary roles.

The Starstreak missile, regardless of which mounting is used, has a common launch tube and a two stage motor. The missile is accelerated away from the canister by the first stage motor which is jettisoned at launch. At a safe distance, the second stage motor ignites and boosts the missile up to many times the speed of sound. On burn out, three darts separate and are guided to the target under the control of the aimer. The use of kinetic and chemical energy darts significantly increases the chance of achieving a kill on the target.

The technology embodied in Starstreak can be utilised in naval defence and Shorts are carrying out a study for the Royal Navy to evaluate applications of the Starstreak technology for naval point defence. The new variant, Seastreak, would enable the requirements of a very short range naval air defence system for the 21st century, to be realised in advance of other competing systems. Its prime characteristic would be to provide a CIWS at a much lower cost than fast firing guns, and in this way it continues the objective of Shorts to produce effective weapons at greatly reduced prices. This is an important aim for technology now growing in significance for all navies.

The various means of controlling Seacat engagements are illustrated in Figure 6.2 and a Seacat missile being fired from a multiple shipboard launcher is shown in Figure 6.3. The general appearance of the Seastreak missile with its three darts is shown in Figure 6.4.

7

Area Defence Missiles

Area defence systems use medium range tactical missiles capable of engaging air or surface targets over a wide area out to ranges of some 100 miles. They can thus provide protection to a group of ships, and in this respect they differ significantly from point defence missiles which provide self protection only for the ship which carries them. Area defence missiles are therefore part of the concept of naval force, as opposed to single ship, operations and they are usually associated with specialist ship roles to provide area air defence. In the Royal Navy the Type 42 destroyers were conceived primarily as area air defence ships to provide this type of cover for a composite force.

In the doctrine of layered defence, the area defence missile provides the second outermost ring of cover inside the outer ring of aircraft cover from 'organic' aircraft carried by the force. Two prime examples of this type of missile are the British Sea Dart and the American Standard missile, both of which have a medium or long range capability. In designing this type of missile system, the main problem and expense lies not so much in the missile as in the associated sensor system for targeting and guidance over a long range. There is no great problem in designing and producing a missile with a long range but, even with airborne assistance, shipborne radars, to detect and classify valid targets at long range are complex, heavy and expensive. This is mainly due to the need to have an adequate multiple target handling capability to counter saturation attacks, and to have a fast response to enable the missiles to be launched in time to engage fast attacking targets, aircraft or missiles, at long ranges. As already explained, targets which get through this ring of defence are taken by the point defence missiles and the close-in weapons, which are usually fast-firing guns. The sensor complexity of area defence missile systems inevitably tended to make these radars large, expensive and heavy, so design attention was concentrated on light weight area systems which will be discussed further below.

Recently, with the need to protect merchant ships and Fleet Auxiliaries, which was made evident in the Falklands War and in the Persian Gulf, there is a perceived requirement for a new type of shorter range area defence known as support defence. This is a missile system which is really a type of extended point defence with a range and sensor system capable of providing self defence for the ship fitted and also providing nearby ships in company with a defence mainly against anti-ship missiles. Such a support defence missile is considerably more expensive than a point defence system and this, coupled with the need to commit a complete warship to carry it, may perhaps make this method of defending ships in company economically less attractive than arming them with self-defence weapon systems. However, this is one of the current issues in the field of naval surface weapons which is now being examined and the outcome will depend not so much on technical weapon system capabilities as on cost. Today's technology can provide virtually any weapon system performance that may be desired; the dominant limitation is cost and ship installation implications, which is really another cost factor.

To illustrate the area defence missile, the British Aerospace Sea Dart is an excellent example of performance and versatility in design variants.

SEA DART

The Sea Dart system has a dual role against both air and surface targets and is suitable, in its GWS30 form, for installation in warships of 3000 tons or more displacement. It has a range in excess of 30 km against air targets and out to the radio horizon against ships. The warhead is of the continuous rod form and has a large kill radius.

Sea Dart has been in service with the Royal Navy since 1973. It was used in combat by the Royal Navy in the Falklands campaign, during which it destroyed seven hostile aircraft. Trials have confirmed the accuracy and lethality of Sea Dart against all types of target—whether aircraft or ships. Sea Dart GWS30 systems are in operational service aboard HMS Bristol and Royal Navy Type 42 destroyers. The Royal Navy's Invincible class of ASW aircraft carriers is also equipped with Sea Dart GWS30.

Sea Dart consists of a ramjet-powered missile to which is attached a tandem-mounted solid-propellant boost motor which is jettisoned when the boost burns out. The missile is guided throughout its sustained flight by a highly accurate, semi-active homing head which enables miss distances of a few metres to be achieved against airborne targets. The continuous rod warhead is triggered by a radio proximity fuse.

The complete missile is 4.35 metres long, of which the boost section accounts for 1.0 metres.

The missile has a cruciform wing and a rear-mounted control fin layout. Four flip-out fins at the rear end of the boost section provide stabilisation during the boost

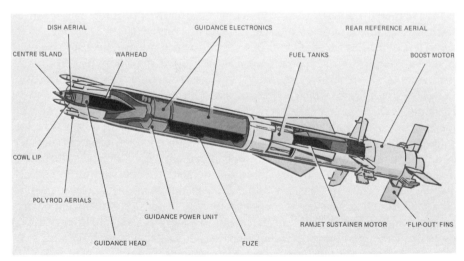

Fig. 7.1   Main features of Sea Dart Missile. (*British Aerospace*)

phase. A central duct conveys ram air down the centre of the missile to the sustainer motor at the rear of the missile. At the front of the missile, an island core in the ram air inlet houses the guidance head and the warhead. The auto-pilot, control electronics, fuse and fuel tanks are all in the annular space between the central air duct and the outer skin of the missile. At each end of the boost motor are the front and rear shoes which mate the missile with the launch rail in the box and which bear the weight of the missile with its boost.

The Sea Dart missile uses semi-active, continuous-wave radar homing guidance. Prior to launch the dish aerial in the front of the missile is tilted to look at a point which is calculated to be the position of the target relative to the missile at the end of the boost phase. After boost separation, the missile guidance head acquires the target and the missile homes on to the reflected illumination signal, following a proportional navigation law.

FIG. 7.2   Sea Dart launcher on board HMS *Illustrious*. (*Photo: British Aerospace*)

Fig. 7.3   Sea Dart firing. (*Photo: British Aerospace*)

To provide a reference for the doppler velocity gate in the missile and a channel for in-flight commands, a portion of the illuminator power is radiated from a wide-beam secondary antenna on the ship and is received by the rear reference aerial in the rear of the missile.

When a target detected by a ship's surveillance radar and confirmed as hostile is to be engaged by the Sea Dart GWS30 system, the tracker illuminator radar associated with the system is directed to acquire the target. The Sea Dart launcher is pointed in the target's direction and, when it is within range, a missile is fired. The boost motor accelerates the missile to a supersonic speed exceeding Mach 2 and before it burns out, the ram-jet motor will be alight and running. After burn out the boost separates and the ram-jet motor sustains the missile's high flight speed until target interception. The Sea Dart warhead detonates on impact or is triggered to explode by a radar proximity fuse. Reloading is automatic and rapid. Ships equipped with two tracker illuminator radars can engage two targets simultaneously.

Guidance and control are by semi-active monopulse radar and the target is illuminated by continuous-wave radar from the launch ship. Sea Dart has four protruding dielectric antennas called polyrods. The orientation of signals reflected by the target can be determined with great precision by these and the missile follows a proportional navigation course to intercept the target. Operated by hydraulically-powered actuators, movable fins at the rear of the missile control flight. Fixed wings are attached to the missile's centre body.

When fired as an anti-ship missile, Sea Dart follows an up and over trajectory, climbing steeply after launch and descending equally steeply onto the target during the final phase of its flight. The kinetic energy built up by the missile on its downward path ensures that the missile penetrates the armoured decks of a target ship to cause extensive internal damage both above and below the waterline. Aboard ship Sea Dart is handled as a round of ammunition, no testing or maintenance being required.

The main features of the missile construction are shown in Figure 7.1. A Sea Dart on its twin launchers on HMS *Illustrious* is seen in Figure 7.2 and a missile firing is shown in Figure 7.3.

LIGHTWEIGHT SEA DART

Possibly of greater interest is the Lightweight Sea Dart system which is a modified form of the original GWS30 arrangement. This is capable of being fitted in quite small ships and providing them with an area defence capability. It consists of standard Sea Dart missiles in deck-mounted launchers, together with a lightweight radar and fire control system.

The Lightweight Sea Dart System retains the anti-ship capability of GWS30 and a large proportion of that system's anti-aircraft and anti-missile capability. In addition, it is suitable for small vessels down to about 300 tons—such as 50 metre fast patrol boats—vessels which are fitted with less heavy but less powerful radars. The system is also an effective weapon fit for much larger ships in either its basic or in its expanded form. It is suitable for retro-fitting as well as fitting in ships of new build.

Lightweight Sea Dart is effective against airborne targets—aircraft, missiles and helicopters—as well as surface targets—ships and hovercraft. A fit of Lightweight Sea Dart avoids the complexity and the logistic problems of fitting and operating the two weapon systems which would otherwise be needed to provide the same operational capability.

A simpler and lighter method of launching is employed, together with a lightweight tracker illuminator radar. Each Sea Dart is housed in a specially-designed sealed box that protects the missile during handling and storage and serves as a launcher when mounted on a ship's deck. Typically, Sea Dart launcher boxes would be mounted on the deck of a small ship, such as a Fast Patrol Boat, in two groups of four, one group facing starboard and the other to port, to meet threats from either quarter. Larger ships could, of course, carry more launcher boxes. During the target tracking phase of an engagement, the missile fire control computer produces ship steering data to bring the selected Sea Dart box onto a suitable bearing for launching the missile.

Sea Dart in its launcher box requires no maintenance or testing on board ship and has a storage life of two years at sea before re-testing at an armament depot ashore is necessary.

The Lightweight Sea Dart box launcher is compatible with the Sea Eagle SL box launcher, both use identical deck mountings, thus light naval craft can be armed with a mix of both weapons appropriate to the particular missions on which they are engaged.

In particular, Lightweight Sea Dart can:

> Inflict critical damage on a surface unit at greater ranges than modern naval guns.
>
> Destroy supersonic or subsonic aircraft at high or low altitude, at extended ranges.
>
> Defend against sub-surface, surface or air-launched missile attacks.
>
> Destroy helicopters in either the attack or surveillance roles.

The system's medium range anti-ship capability, combined with its area defence anti-aircraft capability, makes it an attractive primary weapon fit for small ships down to below 300 tons. Lightweight Sea Dart can also be fitted to larger ships either as a primary or secondary weapon fit. Additional trackers and launchers can be included as required, enabling two targets to be engaged at once.

The lightweight system can thus replace anti-ship and anti-air weapon systems which would otherwise be required to provide the same capability. It provides a significant reduction in overall complexity of the ship weapon fit and the logistics support required.

As we have seen, missiles are stored in and fired from launch boxes, mounted in groups of two or four on bases fixed in azimuth and elevation (20 degrees) and located in convenient positions on the ship's deck. The missile setting equipment, which is concerned with missile selection, warm-up power supplies, signal conversion and firing sequence, is situated as close as is possible to the launcher.

The Sea Dart control console is concerned with engagement feasibility, the prediction of the missile launch window, the anticipated intercept point, calculation of missile settings and the sequence decision logic. It uses the Sperry Gyroscope 1412AL digital processor.

The Tracking and Illuminating Radar (TIR) uses the Marconi Radar ST805, which combines the ST800 series Tracking Radar with the Illuminating Radar from the Sea Dart GWS30 system. The ST805 utilises a 1.4 metre dish.

The engagement sequence is as follows:

> The surveillance system detects and classifies the threat.
>
> The Action Information Organisation allocates targets to the Lightweight Sea Dart System which selects a launcher and indicates the ship's heading required for an engagement.
>
> The Command decision is made to engage.
>
> The TIR receives positional information on the selected target from the ship's surveillance radar, it acquires and locks onto the target and begins tracking.
>
> The control computer receives ship platform positional data and the fire control computation takes place.
>
> Missiles are warmed up.
>
> The Sea Dart illuminator is switched to alert.
>
> The Missile Setting Equipment sets and tunes the missile.
>
> The missile is launched as soon as the launch window is open.
>
> The Sea Dart illuminator begins to radiate.

Missile homing begins at the end of the boost phase. The missile acquires both the radar reflections from the target and the flight control signals from the ship.

The target is destroyed and the next target can be selected. The operation of the system in relation to the missile guidance and target illumination is illustrated in Figure 7.4.

In general the performance of the system is determined by the range capability of the surveillance and tracking radars and, for low level targets, the height of the radar antennae above the sea surface. The diagram gives an indication of the creditable performance that the system achieves with small, lightweight, tracking radars aboard a small vessel.

The diagram in Figure 7.5 illustrates interception brackets for targets approaching along the line of fire of the missile. These interception brackets define the ranges between which the target can be destroyed. Reasonable assumptions have been made about radar performance and disposition in producing the diagram, which is based on a tracking radar having the 1.4 metre diameter dish already described. Improved performance can result if a radar with enhanced capability is used with a bigger dish.

The reaction time for the Sea Dart missile is short. Missile warm-up can be initiated once the surveillance data are available and is completed in the same order of time as the tracker acquisition and lock-on. A warmed-up missile can be fired soon after receipt of valid tracking data on the computer.

The missile is effective against manoeuvring and crossing targets, enabling the Lightweight Sea Dart system to provide an area defence capability to even the smallest vessels in which it is fitted.

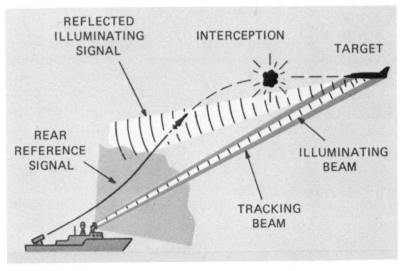

Fig. 7.4   Sea Dart operation in relation to missile guidance and target illumination. (*British Aerospace*)

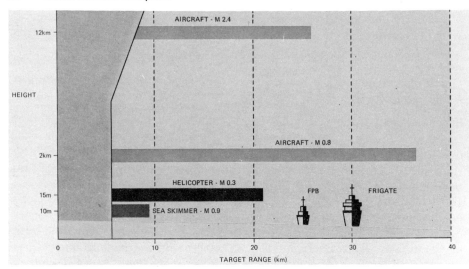

Fɪɢ. 7.5   Lightweight Sea Dart target interception range brackets. (*British Aerospace*)

SUPPORT DEFENCE MISSILE SYSTEM

British Aerospace are giving consideration in current studies to a support defence missile system which will provide a type of area defence over a relatively short range and is primarily concerned with countering attacks of anti-ship sea skimmers against ships in close company. It will provide a layer of air defence for lesser armed ships in company and also self defence for the ship to which it is fitted. The main features will be a high rate of fire, probably from a vertical launcher to counter multiple simultaneous engagements, high agility in the missile and an ability to engage even the most difficult targets. However, as mentioned above, the future of a weapon system of this type will depend primarily on cost. A major step up in cost occurs when the system design moves from self defence to area defence and the basic question is whether or not it would be more cost-effective in all respects to add self protection to the ships concerned. This is discussed further in the next chapter where the question of 'boxed' or 'containerised' defence systems for merchant ships is considered.

8

Merchant Ships as Weapon Platforms

An interesting debate centres on the protection of merchant ships and Fleet Auxiliaries which are either carrying important cargo, as in the present situation in the Persian Gulf, or acting in support of warships, as occurred during the Falklands War. Basically, the issue is whether to arm the civilian ships with their own defensive weapons, to provide warships to protect them, or to engage in a measure of both methods. The question is mainly one of cost, but questions of risk are also involved if merchant ships are fitted with fully automatic weapons in an environment where friendly aircraft and helicopters are operating. Command and control of active weapon systems can not always be left totally to software without experienced men to activate or inhibit the automatic systems.

The question has been addressed, and answered, in the case of some Royal Fleet Auxiliaries where the AOR (Auxiliary Oiler and Replenishment) ships and the ASS (Aviation Support Ships) will have a weapon fit and a complement of operators to run and maintain it. This weapon system will be permanently built into the ships and will give them quite a considerable measure of air defence and communications capability. While this solution is not inexpensive, it could well be the most cost effective but it does involve a permanent weapon fit and the manpower needed for a complement of experienced operators and maintainers.

For merchant ships taken up from trade for naval support work in times of tension or conflict, or for merchant ships carrying valuable strategic cargo a different solution is needed. If warships are used to protect them, the warships must stay in close company, ahead or astern of the merchant ship, to be able to detect a sea skimming missile coming in on either beam. The warship will be able to do little or nothing else and it will need a missile with an area defence capability such as a Support Defence Missile System provides; this is considerably more expensive than a PDMS such as SEAWOLF. Thus, an entire frigate with an expensive missile system could be tied up in the defence of one merchant ship. This is certainly a costly solution, and while it might be justified on particular occasions, there is clearly a case for examining other solutions that could be adopted for the protection of merchant ships. One solution is to provide containerised or boxed weapons that could be put on board merchant ships where required, and also containers of various kinds to enable helicopters or VTOL aircraft to be operated from merchant ships. British Aerospace has given considerable attention to this problem.

The use of merchant ships in a military role in times of defence emergency has been a feature in the history of Britain. More recently, with the introduction of container ships, a new avenue has opened making it possible for kits of containers already fitted with defence equipment to be stored at strategic ports for lifting onto ships at short notice when necessary. In this way, flight decks and hangars may be added to permit the operation of Harrier aircraft, helicopters and protective air defence missiles such as Seawolf. It is from this situation that a term SCADS has emerged standing for Shipborne Containerised Air Defence Systems.

SCADS is a concept for rapidly converting merchant vessels, and unarmed naval auxiliaries into fighting ships in times of national crisis by equipping them with containerised weapon systems plus the necessary operational facilities. Originally conceived for converting merchant ships to the air defence role, the SCADS concept has been enlarged and several different versions have been proposed. Offensive as well as defensive weapons can be fitted. In addition to air defence and helicopter support, armed logistic supply and amphibious assault ships could be commissioned in this way.

A number of container ships were converted to a military role at the time of the Falklands campaign, though the short time available and the absence of pre-equipped military containers limited the extent of the conversions.

Commercial transportation and shipment using ISO containers has now become a familiar sight, because of the relative ease with which pre-loaded containers may be moved overland by truck and stacked onto ships at container terminals using minimum manpower. The term ISO is an abbreviation for International Standards Organisation which for containers defines standard features such as dimensions and fixings so that containers will fit all container ships and the container terminal handling equipment. The cross sectional dimensions are 8 ft by 8.5 ft, with a choice in length of 10, 20 and 40 ft, the latter two being the most used in SCADS applications. These containers are located one above each other in the ship's holds. Above deck they are stacked up to three or four high, being held to the deck and to each other by quick-operation twistlocks at the corners; lashing bars are usually added to provide extra security. To enable merchant ships to undergo quick conversion under the SCADS principle and yet remain in trade, it is necessary to adopt the standard container dimensions and fixings, though the structure of the equipment units within these containers may be modified for added security and where localised heavy equipment is fitted.

A containerised weapon comprises a set of standard ISO containers in which are housed all the equipment facilities needed for the autonomous operation of the weapon. Containerised weapons are assembled, system integration completed and all functional checks performed in the factory prior to delivery to the dockside where they can be quickly installed aboard ships. Each ship can be equipped with a selection of weapons appropriate to its immediate operational role.

Following service, the containerised weapon systems can be removed equally quickly to reinstate the ship to its former commercial role. Or following action, the containerised weapons can be removed for servicing, or repair, and replaced by refurbished systems to maintain the fighting capability of the ship.

British Aerospace weapons for which containerised configurations have been devised include the Seawolf point-defence anti-missile missile, the dual role light-weight Sea Dart anti-aircraft and anti-ship missile, and the ship-launched Sea Eagle SL anti-ship missile.

A containerised gun has been designed. A typical installation would comprise a BMARC twin 30 mm GCM gun and an electro-optical fire director mounted on top of the container, with a Sea Archer weapon control system inside.

A typical autonomous Seawolf system could be accommodated in five standard ISO containers. A tracking radar would be mounted on top of the container equipped with the radar electronics. Another container would be fitted-out as the weapon operations room, and another would house the necessary system power generators. The remaining two containers would be used as magazines for Seawolf with a missile launcher mounted on top of each. Or the containers could house vertically launched Seawolf missiles in their launch canisters. Other defence equipment could be provided in containerised form, such as surveillance radars, decoy and counter-measures systems and AIO rooms. A flight deck from which helicopters and Sea Harriers would be able to operate could be supported on containers. Furthermore, the additional living accommodation and services needed for the extra crew that would be required could be provided in containers.

As prime contractor, British Aerospace has completed one project of this type. It was the conversion of the 23,000 tonne containership *Astronomer* into the Royal Fleet Auxiliary helicopter support ship *Reliant*. The conversion involved the installation of 74 containers. Those for helicopter operation came from a prototype system known as Arapaho and provided fueling services, flying control, stores facilities and mechanical and electrical workshops. Other containers provided crew living accommodation including water and sewage facilities, galleys, mess areas, laundry, NAAFI and food stores. Shortly after completion, RFA *Reliant* was deployed on active service in the Mediterranean in support of a British land force.

Containerised weapons for naval vessels have been proposed and British Aerospace has a technical agreement with Blohm and Voss relating to the MEKO container design of naval ship construction being developed by that company.

RFA *Reliant* had demonstrated the potential of containerisation, and provided a helicopter support ship within nine months at low cost, enabling the capabilities of the Fleet to be extended at a time of need. This had been a conversion basically from scratch and so took time to complete. If, however, kits of containers are designed in advance and then fitted-out and stored, ship conversions can be made much more quickly. This concept, known as Arapaho, had, in fact been to have available a set of containers and flight deck modules already designed, equipped and maintained in working order, ready to be fitted to a ship in time of emergency to allow helicopters or aircraft to travel with the ship and provide defence from attack. In principle the ship could still carry much of its normal cargo.

British Aerospace has more recently undertaken studies on how to achieve quick conversions, and set itself the target of designing a system which would permit conversion on a pre-prepared ship within two to seven days. To achieve quick connection of cables and pipes between containers, and without a need for scaffolding, a service gallery at the end of each container is proposed. Pre-fitted and tested sections of cables and pipes in these galleries would be connected at installation in the ship, using electrical connectors and quick-fit pipe couplings and flexible bellows. Cutaways in walls between containers would be limited to small areas and would be pre-fitted with concertina type seals.

Provided the containers have been assembled together previously and tested on a

FIG. 8.1   Helicopter support ship RFA *Reliant*. Converted from 23,000 tonne container
ship. (*British Aerospace*)

land site and the installation personnel trained at the site, it is considered that the
installation in the ship can be made in seven days. To minimise modifications to the
ship, all containers are fitted above deck, and it is estimated that the ship modification
could then be completed in a three week period, such as at a normal maintenance
docking time. The ship may remain in trade for most of the time, with the Flight
Support System fitted for short or long periods when and if necessary. It is possible
to consider repeated fits over a period of 10 years.

The advantages of SCADS conversions, resulting from the ease of handling and
transporting containers may be summarised as follows:

Quick-fit weapon installation using prepared kits in merchant and naval ships
in time of emergency.
Short term conversion of a merchant ship when prepared kits are not
available.
Containers can be moved by road to the chosen installation port.
Commercial container terminals can be used for loading.
Loading can also be undertaken at other ports.
Dispersed storage away from shipyards can be adopted.
Flexibility by substitution of containers.

Merchant ships can remain in trade between fits and still achieve much of their cargo carriage when SCADS is fitted.

Distributed manufacture offers a wider choice of manufacturers.

The skilled work of installing and checking equipment within the containers is undertaken in controlled conditions at specialist factories, rather than alongside the heavier work on the ship.

Conversions can be undertaken by countries not having complex ship building facilities.

If, however, a long term conversion is required and one is not limited to the container handling facilities, then an extension of containerisation can be used where large modules weighting 150 to 200 tons are pre-fitted and then lifted onto the ship. In such a situation the accommodation block and hangar would each perhaps be two modules, which would be welded together on the ship. The ship modifications required are more extensive than with ISO containers, and the handling of the large items restricts the locations where installations can be made. This is a more permanent conversion and, for instance, includes lifts to a below-deck hangar. The accommodation block is also below deck. Such a ship could operate six Harrier aircraft and three helicopters with a runway 120 metres long by 16 metres wide and a 12 degree ski-jump.

An arrangement of containerised weapons would certainly be a flexible and versatile method of providing protection for merchant ships. As a national strategic investment which could be stored when not required it could well be more cost effective than the provision of warships which would have to have an anti-missile system with greater range and capability than a normal PDMS; such a support or area defence missile system is in itself an expensive capability to provide.

9

The Way Ahead

GENERAL TRENDS

The way ahead for naval surface weapons is inevitably linked with the future of surface warships as well as being strongly influenced by the trends of modern weapon technology. So far as surface ships are concerned, their role in military and naval operations as instruments for effecting political policy is likely to be governed by at least two important factors: their unique suitability for various tasks and their cost-effectiveness, which includes their vulnerability to attack as well as their inherent capabilities.

So long as large quantities of materials and men can best, if not only, be transported by sea then the traditional naval role of escorting and protecting surface transports and merchant ships from submarine and air attacks will remain. This task of keeping open the important sea lanes and routes is one for which surface ships are uniquely fitted, assisted, as necessary, by submarines and aircraft. There is no real sign of this naval function changing; nothing else could perform it so appropriately as surface warships. Coupled with this, is a number of other roles in which surface ships have played, and can play a very useful part, such as gunfire support for military operations ashore, policing duties and diplomatic functions. It is appropriate to consider what are the prime and important characteristics of surface warships as weapon carriers, and here one factor is of outstanding importance; the surface warship can carry a much larger and heavier payload than an aircraft, satellite or submarine, although the latter are now becoming very large themselves. However, the large weapon payload and capacity for long endurance which characterise the surface ship are both of great importance in terms of its offensive and defensive capability. Indeed, these unique and highly significant features will govern not only the future of the surface ship itself but of naval surface weapons also.

The cost and cost effectiveness of surface warships as weapon carriers will continue to be major determining factors in the selection of their future roles. It has always been so in the past but their significance has increased as modern technology has made it possible to incorporate weapons and sensors of very great cost in the design of new ships. Even though the increase in the cost effectiveness of the weapon systems overall has been substantial, so too has been the increase of cost—and absolute cost, rather than cost effectiveness, is often the determining factor when equipment policy is being decided. If surface warships cannot be adequately effective in terms of their weapon capability for an acceptable cost, the future of the surface warship must be in doubt and other means of implementing the political policy involved must be sought. Thus when we consider the future of surface warships and their weapons it must be in terms of their *absolute* cost in relation to the provision of an *acceptable* capability in offence and defence.

The cost of a ship's hull, propulsion units and ancillary marine equipment does not change very markedly; the real cost determinant lies in the weapons and sensors needed to keep a ship viable. There is, after all, not much point in having a superb anti-submarine search and destroy capability (which needs to be carried out in a surface ship, because of its weight), if the ship is inadequately protected from air or missile attack. The cost of adequate air defence for the warship must be acceptable. Similarly, an effective air defence is of little value if the ship is vulnerable to underwater attack. Although it was once naval policy to have specialised ships for particular roles so that a mix enabled a group of ships—whether a task group or a fleet—to have a balanced weapon capability overall, the Falklands and other experience have taught us that each ship must, in itself, have an overall weapon balance. This is a very costly business indeed and must limit severely the number of warships a nation can afford, regardless of the number actually required to execute national policies—so that, logically, this situation must influence a nation's ability to sustain its policies and so tends to govern the scope of those policies also.

This line of argument leads to the general conclusion that the future of naval surface weapons, and indeed the future of surface ships, is likely to be influenced strongly, if not determined, by the extent to which absolute cost can be controlled and reduced in the design and development of adequately effective weapon systems. Certainly, at present, the cost factor, rather than the performance, is dominant in the sales of naval surface weapons by the supply industry. Technology today has no difficulty in producing almost any weapon performance which might be desired—at a price. The major challenge to the weapon system designers is to reduce costs, not to increase the performance. They may seek to do this through modularity, which is really designing one piece of equipment to do several tasks. They may seek to do it by replacing men, who are very expensive in a warship, with software control and automation. They may seek to use less costly, but adequately effective devices such as guided projectiles rather than guided missiles. In short, whatever methods are employed, they really must produce a marked reduction in cost if naval surface weapons and ships are to continue to play an important and significant part in future as instruments of political policies.

This is a difficult but by no means impossible task for the naval weapon industry. It requires a different attitude to weapon design since there still lingers the inherent objective from World War II days that each new generation of weapon system must have a higher performance; now the prime objective must be a lower cost to halt or reverse the escalation in weapon expenditure. Certain trends in technology can help in this, such as the falling costs of data processing, which should aid the reduction in the costs of automation. But other trends, such as supersonic sea-skimming missiles, will inevitably bring much more difficult problems and possibly higher costs, in air defence. Nevertheless, the challenge to the weapon designers to reduce overall weapon system costs is there, and it will be interesting to see in the future how well it has been met. A design trend towards lower overall costs is already beginning in, for example, modularity and guided projectiles but this needs to gain more momentum.

GUNS, AUTOMATION AND NEW WEAPONS

To be somewhat more specific in considering the way ahead for naval surface weapons, three likely trends may be discerned which will influence the types of weapon system over the next several decades. First, there is likely to be a continuing need for relatively simple, manually operated guns for policing and patrol duties, and for general surface and air actions against minor threats. Guns of this type in service today are most likely to continue in their present form. Coupled with this, is a requirement for some larger guns of around 5 inch calibre, specifically for naval gunfire support ashore. This represents a recovery of the priority awarded to naval gunfire which is likely to be a feature of some, but not necessarily all, classes of frigate. So guns will probably continue with greater rather than less importance, especially if current work on precision guided projectiles is successful in creating a lower cost naval weapon with enough accuracy over medium ranges to have some anti-missile capability, particularly against the sea skimmers of today's generation.

Second, with the increasing pace of naval engagements, due to supersonic anti-ship missiles, there is likely to be a firm trend towards more completely automatic weapons for air defence. These weapon systems, using fast-firing guns, missiles or precision guided projectiles will be software controlled. In effect, the significant change is going to be the growth of software control, with its corresponding effect on the man–machine relationship in naval weapons. The part played by the man in future is likely to be as an inhibitor, rather than an initiator of weapon system operation. He will switch off a weapon if he thinks it is attacking or about to attack a friendly target; but the initial choice of target and the initiation of the weapon system operation will be by software. The software will, of course, be written by a man in the first instance. This changed role of the man in surface ships is significant for his training and represents one of the major changes that will come about in the future. To achieve greater economy in naval weaponss, these automatic systems are likely to be modular in design and to employ one set of sensors and data processors to control two or more weapons, such as a point defence missile and a fast-firing CIWS gun. Already, this type of change is in sight with such far-seeing companies as Contraves and is a definite pointer for the future.

Third, there is the possibility if not probability that future surface weapon systems in ships may employ totally new kinds of beam-type weapon, such as high power lasers or electromagnetic rail launchers, and multiple launched rocket systems. The essential link between these weapons and ships is that a surface warship has the capability of carrying the heavy payload involved (typically 20 tonnes) for a high energy laser. They are much more suitable for ships than for aircraft or satellites. Their naval application is being considered as they offer an attractive multiple target capability against saturation attacks using lasers and electromagnetic launchers, and a powerful shore bombardment capability out to some 30 kilometres using multiple rocket launchers. High energy lasers are reasonably well known and the type appropriate for use as weapons are chemical lasers which derive their energy from a chemical reaction; their fuel is a relatively common chemical. While they do give the possibility of being able to provide rapid and successive shots, making them very suitable for point defence in a saturation attack, they too are heavy (again, some 20 tonnes) and may be seriously affected by the atmosphere. This can cause beam bending and a dilution of energy in the shots, due to diffusion and de-focussing of the beam. Nevertheless, high energy lasers do offer an important potential as naval weapons against missiles and aircraft and may very well find a place in naval weapon systems of the future. Atmospheric degradation is their principal drawback for naval use and it remains to be seen whether or not they can be designed to provide enough energy in the atmosphere to give an adequate measure of point defence against missiles. The electromagnetic rail launcher is, perhaps, less well known. It is a method of accelerating projectiles to very high velocities of the order of 20 km/s and is being investigated in Europe and in the United States. While work is still at an early stage, it is possible that a system capable of operating in the atmosphere in a point defence role against missiles and aircraft may be practicable. The basic attraction of the electromagnetic launcher is accuracy. With such an extremely high muzzle velocity, the time of flight of the projectiles will be very short and fire control prediction errors will be reduced to an acceptable level. The cost is a large payload weight and the large volume of space on board ship required to accommodate the weapon. Currently, only surface ships can carry these weapons.

The multiple launch rocket system (MLRS) can provide a salvo of, typically, 12 rockets repeated within less than 1 minute. At a range of some 30 kilometres it can provide a type of area bombardment said to be more effective than that from a 5 inch gun. Of course each rocket could produce a large number of 50 or more bomblets capable of piercing tank top armour and these bomblets could later be terminally guided to their targets. Altogether the MLRS provides a relatively inexpensive weapon of formidable performance which is heavy and suitable for surface ships. It is perhaps the most effective and least costly device for naval gunfire support ashore and is clearly a possible future naval surface weapon; as such we must include it in this survey.

For naval gunfire support ashore MLRS may well fulfill the criterion of lower cost weapons with adequate effectiveness which was discussed earlier in this chapter, because it uses inexpensive engineering techniques. Compared with, for example, the 5″ gun of today, which is essentially a construction of expensive precision engineering to produce an accurate weapon. The MLRS uses more inexpensive, non-precision engineering techniques and provides a devastating bombardment over a small area without the high precision in accuracy of the gun. Thus it sacrifices pinpoint accuracy for economy. Where this is acceptable in bombardment tasks, the MLRS may prove to be a better solution in giving a lower absolute cost with an adequate and acceptable performance in accuracy, coupled, possibly, with a high destructive capability in the area where the projectiles fall. As we have seen, such considerations of cost and effectiveness are going to play a very important part in the assessment of future naval surface weapon systems in which the overall composition of a ship's weapon systems is being defined. Will a shotgun suffice rather than an automatic rifle for certain tasks?

HIGHER RELIABILITY AND TOTAL WEAPON SYSTEMS

Another strong influence on the selection of naval surface weapons of the future is the advantage to be gained from higher reliability. Apart from improved performance through better availability, which is always welcome, higher assured reliability

FIG. 9.1   The elegant lines of the Libyan frigate *DAT Assawari*, built by Vosper Thorney-croft and armed with Otomat and Albatros Missiles and 4.5 inch, 35 millimetre and 20 millimetre guns. (*Photo: Naval Forces*)

could lead to the need for less 'maintainers' to go to sea in the ships. This would produce a marked economy, as men living in ships are expensive in their accommodation, messing and training. To achieve a higher reliability can lead back to the methods of weapon procurement and the means of making reliability a contractual obligation.

Many attempts have been made to achieve, or enforce, reliability in naval weapons through some form of contractual obligation. In general, all have failed. This has been for various reasons but primarily because of the difficulty of attributing unreliability to a design fault or weakness as opposed to misuse or maltreatment of the equipment by the user. However, new processes of procurement by what is known as the Cardinal Points method offers a more realistic solution in inviting competition for a measure of equipment performance over a stated period of, say, five years. In these circumstances, the contractor would bid for the supply of the equipment and its maintenance within a single fixed price. He is thus strongly motivated to employ a design of equipment with adequate in-built reliability which is considered from the very beginning of the design process. Only through this form of contractual relationship and attitude to reliability is it at all likely that a real advance will be made in the achievement of a much higher degree of reliability than is now to be found in most naval weapon systems. For too long, the emphasis has been placed upon higher performance. One of the primary aims in future must be the achievement of a reduction in the number of maintenance crewmen needed on board. This is only likely to be achieved if reliability becomes a principal requirement when the procurement package is drawn up for competition.

Another trend in future naval surface weapon system design is rooted in the methods of procurement of warships. Ships are now being made the subject of fixed price competitions involving the entire vessel, including its hull, propulsion, marine equipments and weapons. To respond to this procedure, the prime contractors in industry are using a number of major sub-contractors to design and specify parts of the warship. One of these is known as the Ship Weapon System Authority (SWSA) and has the responsibility of designing, specifying, assembling, testing and installing the entire weapon system. So, instead of weapons and sensors being bought entirely separately, following a design process which considered them in isolation, they are likely to be procured in future by the sub-contractor SWSA or as a complete system,

FIG. 9.2   The Royal Netherlands Navy's Guided Weapons Destroyer *Tromp*. (*Photo: Naval Forces*)

following a design process in which they have been considered and created as part of a single weapon system. This procurement process has many potential advantages in that it can lead to better economy through common modular units serving more than one function and to improved mutual compatibility and interoperability of the equipments which make up the system. In this way a greater unity and homogeneity in weapon system design may be gained, to the advantage of naval operations.

On the whole, the naval surface weapons of the future are likely to be dominated in influence by the need to give protection, self and mutual, against the most significant probable threat to surface ships. In all likelihood, this will be the saturation attack from supersonic anti-ship missiles which may have a sea-skimming, a high dive at steep angles, or a manoeuvring capability. The combination of saturation attacks, requiring multiple channels of fire for defence, high speed anti-ship missiles requiring very fast reaction in defence and 'intelligent' homing heads to counter simple EW poses a very major threat and a great engineering challenge to weapon designers to provide an effective defence. The balance of offensive and defensive capability in naval surface warfare changes over the years and decades in response to advances of technology and naval tactics. At present that balance seems to be in favour of the attack on warships rather than their capability to provide a defence. No doubt this balance will change in time and the image of the invincible and impregnable warship will begin to re-emerge as the effectiveness and nature of naval surface weapons continue to evolve in cycles, as they always have.

FUTURE MISSILES

Since missiles will play a very significant part in future surface weapon systems, it is appropriate to consider the factors influencing their development, and in this respect the views of Aerospatiale are interesting.

Attempting to predict naval armaments and engagements in the years 1995/2000 may seem, at first sight, somewhat pretentious. However, the development of a major weapon project—from the first feasibility studies to the introduction into operational service—spreads out over an eight to ten year period. In consequence, the weapon systems of the coming decade are under preparation today. It is therefore necessary to form a precise idea of the offensive and defensive weapons which might be opposed in a major naval engagement in 1995.

Assessments show that the majority of offensive naval weapons will be missiles; the growing effectiveness of air defence systems becomes strongly dissuasive for conventional air strikes based on bombs and rockets. The Air Forces will use stand-off weapons increasingly and the inventory of offensive weapons will include air-to-surface and surface-to-surface tactical missiles, cruise missiles and short or medium range tactical ballistic missiles. These missiles will in most cases be launched in salvoes in order to saturate enemy defences, making all-round attacks at very short time intervals. All this will occur in a severe jamming environment.

Within this general context, what should be the trend of essential improvements? In view of the progress made by the defensive systems, most efforts should be devoted to increasing penetration capabilities. Quick firing guns and anti-aircraft missiles have partly filled the gap in terms of first generation anti-ship missiles, which have an almost straight trajectory; this applies also to the defence against sea-skimmers, although the latter are still the most difficult targets.

FIG. 9.3   A modern Norwegian Patrol Craft firing the Penguin Missile. (*Photo: Kongsberg*)

The first and most obvious line of progress is increased speed. Higher speed reduces the defence's warning time; it also reduces the time of exposure to enemy fire; in particular, an anti-aircraft missile system will have no time to launch a second missile if the first one has failed.

The second line of progress—the most promising one—concerns the mobility of the attacking missile. This offers a double advantage. First, during the mid-course phase of the trajectory, broad manoeuvres or false approach courses give rise to a state of doubt regarding the actual target and prevent a correct analysis of the threat, thus delaying the defence systems allocation. In the case of a salvo firing, such a method allows pincer movement manoeuvres to be achieved, with simultaneous arrivals of missiles from different directions. Then, during the final phase, progress made in detection and tracking, using combined radar and optronic sensors, give the defending ship a good detection capability out to the horizon (hence the advantage of sea skimming) and an excellent capability of anticipating the attacking missile's future trajectory. In these circumstances, trajectories pre-set to escape such systems should include rapid and random changes of direction in order to elude gun-based defences. Flexible trajectories make the missile less vulnerable to gun-based defence systems, even in the case of subsonic and low manoeuvring missiles. To make progress in these two fields, the aim is to improve the missile thrust either to increase the speed in a straight line or for high load factor manoeuvres with no loss of speed.

The third line of progress covers the reduction of the radar cross-section for the minimum radar echo. There are several available techniques including those using the smallest possible missile diameter, specially designed shapes (suppression of sharp angles and highly reflecting surfaces), and the use of 'transparent' materials or liners. Obviously, any action resulting in late detection is profitable and increases the penetration capabilities. But the reduction of the radar cross-section has limits; in particular, the kinetic heating creates an infra-red signature which adds to the motor signature and this cannot be totally eliminated. Besides, the homing head radar transmission, even if compressed, will be detected. A missile with penetration capabilities based only on 'stealth' features will nevertheless be detected and it will then be vulnerable if it is not capable of complex manoeuvres, all the more so as the defending sensors have made real progress.

There is a fourth significant and even fundamental, line of progress which has a high level of security classification in the resistance of the missile to ECM and decoys. Considerable progress has been made in the effectiveness and rapidity of missile identification sensors and their ability for analysis of the tactical situation.

These general comments give a basis to predict the main features of the future anti-ship missile. Compared to existing systems, improvements will concern the increase of thrust and therefore of speed and load factors. Practically, this will make fast firing guns less effective and the risks of interception by surface to air missiles of the present generation would be considerably reduced.

Application of these new technologies results in the definition of new missile systems, a typical example of which being the Aerospatiale ANS (Supersonic Anti-ship Missile). Its power-plant is a ramjet engine. The ANS is a fire and forget sea skimmer, flying at over Mach 2 and capable of manoeuvres under high load factors. Its conventional range of 180 kilometres requires roughly the same flight time as a 70 kilometre range subsonic missile. The important point is the flight-time,

FIG. 9.4   ASTER—General appearance. (*Artist's impression from Aerospatiale*)

since the size of the homing head search area is connected with the possible movement of the target during the missile flight. In-flight updating is technically possible but it has not been adopted for operational reasons.

In the face of this future threat it is necessary to design an air defence system with a true anti-missile capability, which requires better features than for anti-aircraft warfare. All current attack scenarios call for a first wave of missiles to suppress the defence, aimed first at the radar antennas. There thus exists at least one essential requirement for self defence missile systems.

As they must protect mass saturation attacks, air defence systems must, necessarily, have a multiple target engagement capability. Then they will need to have autonomous or quasi-autonomous missiles to engage a number of targets simultaneously and active homing may be essential.

Given the attacking missiles' high speeds, which can exceed 800 metres per second, whether they be of diving or low altitude type, and given their low electromagnetic signature, interception, which is linked to the detection range, may well be effected only at a short distance from the defended ship, especially in the case of saturation attacks. A system kill is thus not enough, since there is considerable likelihood that a missile of which only the guidance and control have been hit can continue to fly for several kilometres. This risk is not acceptable and the missile must be stopped in its flight and destroyed. A structural kill must be obtained, and this will require a very small miss distance.

Efforts will be made to strengthen attacking missiles and they will be better protected against system kills than against structural kills. For the former it is enough

FIG. 9.5   The price of an inadequate anti-missile defence—the hit of an Exocet. (*Photo: Aerospatiale*)

to protect some major equipments and to build in some functional redundancy. Against structural kill, the protection is more difficult because it leads to a significant mass increase that makes the missile less agile and less manoeuvrable and thus easier to intercept with a short miss distance. Therefore a structural kill is the aim of the anti-missile missile and extreme agility is needed in order to achieve a very small miss distance. For self-guided surface to air missiles, the guidance time constant varies almost linearly with the mass of the missile and thus of its warhead.

With conventional aerodynamic control, the command unit creates a torque which generates a change in the body pitch angle. This, in turn, induces the angle of attack necessary to create the lateral force. This long chain of intermediate steps unavoidably stretches the response time and limits agility. So a different control system is needed. Aerospatiale has developed a novel system based on the use of a pyrotechnic control acting at or near the centre of gravity, combined with a conventional aerodynamic control. This combination, named PIF-PAF, constitutes an homogeneous device which benefits from the advantages inherent in its two components and which minimizes their respective disadvantages. In this control system the lateral force necessary for the missile movement is directly created close to the centre of gravity by hot gas jets. The gas is produced by a gas generator and, through a switch, is directed towards the nozzles corresponding to the desired orientation of the thrust. The response time of this device is typically between 10 and 15 ms. The gain in response time reaches a factor of 10 compared to conventional aerodynamic control.

With the PIF-PAF control system, a powerful method is available to give the defence missile a great manoeuvre capability with a very short response time and thus

Fig. 9.6   The Swedish Navy's first *Spica II* fast patrol boat at speed. Fitted
with the Sea GIRAFFE multipurpose radar. (*Photo: Ericsson Radio Systems
AB/Naval Forces*)

a true anti-missile capability for future agile missiles. Aerospatiale has such a missile
under development. It has two stages:

A terminal dart named ASTER, light and very agile due to PIF-PAF.

A booster capable of putting the ASTER dart in the required interception
domain.

This missile is launched vertically to provide cover from all directions with a very
short reaction time and so to give the defence system an almost simultaneous
engagement capability against multiple targets.

Mid course guidance is provided by an inertial guidance system with an uplink
which updates the target data. After the handover, the guidance is continuous with
aerodynamic pilotage. In the terminal phase, at the best moment, the PIF pilot comes
in to help the PAF so as to insure an accurate interception making it possible to
structurally destroy the target with a warhead of realistic size.

The general appearance of ASTER is shown in Figure 9.4, and the dramatic effect
of the hit of an Exocet which is shown in Figure 9.5 illustrates what can happen if the
net missile defences fail.

The prediction of future trends in the evolution of weapons is always uncertain depending, as it does, on the technical success and cost of new techniques and on the assessment of threats by naval authorities. However, it seems that some, if not all of the factors discussed in this chapter are very likely to play a significant part in shaping some of the naval surface weapons of the future. The evolution of modern weapons is continuous. It is now proceeding at a much faster pace than it ever did before and that pace is increasing.

Self-Test Questions

The questions listed by chapters below are intended to help the student. They have been so framed that the answers may be found without difficulty within the text of the appropriate chapter.

Chapter 1

1.1 Is the choice of weapons a primary or a secondary consideration in the design of warships?

1.2 What are the basic functions and purposes of naval surface weapons?

1.3 What is the principal difference in the assembly of a complement of weapons in a warship now compared with the situation 40 years ago?

1.4 Name some of the major factors which have influenced weapons in modern warships, and explain why and how this influence has developed.

1.5 What is probably the most significant new naval surface weapon in modern times, and why is it so important?

1.6 Is the role of the man in the operation of naval weapons changing?

1.7 In the design of modern naval weapons, how should naval officers and civilian engineers in industry collaborate?

1.8 Consider the basic importance of the Naval Application Officer in weapon design and how this principle could be used more widely in engineering in other fields.

1.9 Why is the method of procurement important for the effectiveness and the cost-effectiveness of naval weapons?

1.10 Is naval fire power totally governed by hull size? What limits apply?

Chapter 2

2.1 Examine some of the principal considerations in planning a naval operation which will involve the use of weapons.

2.2 Why is intelligence information on enemy capabilities so important in planning a naval operation and in weapon design?

2.3 Should the threat assessment for an operation be the responsibility of the officer who will conduct the operation or should it be provided for him?

2.4 Consider the advantages and disadvantages of emission control (radio and radar silence) in naval operations. Why was it so very important in World War II?

2.5 What is your view of the relative importance of weapon capabilities and naval officers' tactical skill in modern warfare? Is the balance changing?

2.6 Explain the principles and advantages of the concept of defence in depth.

2.7 What makes air support so important for naval surface operations?
2.8 Why are multiple channels of fire now so important in modern warships?
2.9 Will missiles ever replace guns? How do you see the role of the naval gun developing in the future?
2.10 With the performance of modern weapons are surface warships viable?

Chapter 3

3.1 In your view, are naval weapons more the result of operational requirements or technological capabilities?
3.2 List some of the more important trends in naval gun technology.
3.3 Why have precision guided munitions become potentially important naval weapons in an age of missiles?
3.4 Consider the ways in which information technology is used in modern naval weapon systems and why it is important.
3.5 Why is a data highway now required in modern warships?
3.6 Naval surface weapons are increasingly being designed as complete systems— why?
3.7 What are the main advantages and any disadvantages in the principle of modularity in weapon system design?
3.8 What advantages and problems are brought by the vertical launching of missiles?
3.9 How is intelligence given to modern weapons and how do they benefit from it?
3.10 Since electronics is now so important in weapon systems, what are the new requirements on electronic components to make them suitable for use in weapons?

Chapter 4

4.1 Why are naval guns now enjoying an increased regard and priority?
4.2 List the main types, characteristics and uses of naval guns.
4.3 Should gun design now be more influenced by lower cost or higher performance?
4.4 Is more accuracy through intelligence in gun systems preferable to more explosive and destructive power from better ammunition?
4.5 What must a CIWS gun achieve to give adequate missile protection?
4.6 What is the purpose and importance of penetrators? How are they designed?
4.7 Examine the advantages and dangers which could be associated with automatically controlled guns.
4.8 What new features would you wish to see in naval guns?
4.9 Should future naval guns be designed for special purposes to gain effectiveness or for general purposes for economy? Discuss.
4.10 How should the naval weapon task be shared between guns and missiles?

Chapter 5

5.1 Why is the sea skimming missile so important as a naval weapon?

5.2 Does the balance of attack and defence effectiveness currently favour the ship or the missile?

5.3 Discuss some of the ways to counter an anti-ship missile.

5.4 Why will increased intelligence in the head of a missile enhance its lethality?

5.5 What is dual sensor homing and why does it give a missile more effectiveness?

5.6 What governs the choice of range in the design of an anti-ship missile?

5.7 How are anti-ship missiles targeted? Give examples.

5.8 Discuss the importance of velocity to a sea-skimmer.

5.9 Describe broadly the main sequences in using an anti-ship missile to attack a target; what does the missile do?

5.10 What are the principal causes of damage to a ship hit by a large anti-ship missile?

Chapter 6

6.1 What is the prime importance of point defence missiles as an element of the defence in depth concept?

6.2 What are the range of types of PDMS and their principal areas of application?

6.3 Why must PDMS be automatic in operation for missile defence?

6.4 What is the role of the man in an automatic missile system?

6.5 What are the additional advantages gained from having point defence missiles vertically launched?

6.6 Compare the main characteristics of Sea Cat and Seastreak with the features of Seawolf.

6.7 Compare the performance and cost of PDMS and naval guns with an anti-missile capability and show how both contribute to defence in depth.

6.8 Describe the principal features of the design of a PDMS. What do you think are its most important aspects?

6.9 How are multiple channels of fire controlled in a warship to ensure the most effective use of ammunition?

6.10 In providing a defence against sea skimmers, what in general terms, is the relative importance of cost, reaction time, agility and range in a point defence missile.

Chapter 7

7.1 What is the role of the area defence missile in a layered defence?

7.2 Should air defence of a ship in company be provided by an air defence missile or by fitting a PDMS or a CIWS in the ship concerned?

7.3 Is the concept of a specialist ship for area air defence, without a full self defence capability, valid in present day naval operations and economically viable?

7.4 Describe the principal elements of the Sea Dart system of radars and missile.

7.5 Discuss the variants possible in area defence missile systems to make them more versatile and cost-effective.

7.6 Why not leave air defence entirely to PDMS and CIWS?

7.7 Why are the radar sensors usually the limiting elements of cost and weight in longer range missile systems?

7.8   What is the status of reliability in major naval weapon systems and how should design be approached to improve it?

7.9   Should all types of shipboard missile have a common magazine and launching facility? What problems and advantages would this bring?

7.10 As an anti-ship weapon compare the effectiveness of the area defence missile, the sea skimmer and the naval gun.

Chapter 8

8.1   Should merchant ships be protected from air attacks by warships or by containerised weapons?

8.2   What are the logistic and cost problems in providing an adequate number of containerised weapons at the main merchant ship ports?

8.3   How should weapons on merchant ships be controlled and operated—by merchant seamen or naval personnel?

8.4   Is the use of a warship fitted with extended range PDMS to protect a merchant ship wasteful of the warship investment?

8.5   Is there a command and control problem in fitting merchant ships with weapons for air defence?

8.6   What are the merits of the SCADS concept?

8.7   What types of weapons and sensors could best be containerised?

8.8   Would purely automatic weapons be suitable for merchant ships?

8.9   How would merchant ships design, operation and procedures have to be altered to accommodate containerised air defence?

8.10 How should the cost factor in providing air defence for merchant ships be assessed and accorded weight in planning for wars at sea?

Chapter 9

9.1   In broad terms, what are the main reasons for a future need for surface warships?

9.2   Why is the absolute cost of surface weapons likely to be of major importance in the future?

9.3   Give three likely trends for the evolution of future naval guns.

9.4   Explain why higher reliability in future weapon systems is of basic importance to the future of warships. How could this be achieved?

9.5   Discuss the total weapon system concept, why it is required and the advantages it can bring.

9.6   Explain why intelligence in future weapons is likely to be a dominant characteristic rather than increased explosive or destructive power.

9.7   Give three likely trends for the evolution of future naval missiles.

9.8   What weapon system characteristicss will be required to counter saturation attacks against ships in the future?

9.9   How is the weapon supply industry likely to evolve to provide naval weapons of the future?

9.10 What aspects of naval weapon design should be carried out within naval establishments rather than by industry?

About the Author

Dr Kiely is a Consultant Engineer following his last appointment in the UK Ministry of Defence as The Chief Naval Weapon System Engineer.

A graduate of Queen's University, Belfast and of the Sorbonne, and a Fellow of the Institutes of Physics and of Electrical Engineering his career has been in the field of marine electronics both for the Royal Navy and for civil marine applications. He has also been much concerned with the methods and organization of large scale defence procurement, and devised and introduced the Cardinal Points Procurement procedure.

Dr Kiely's interests include fly fishing, gardening and the conservation of rare species; he is a member of the World Pheasant Association and a supporter of similar bodies.

Index

Absolute cost   99
Aerospatiale   62
Agility in missiles   22
Albatros   80
ANS missile   67, 105
Anti-ship missiles   57
Application Officers   2
Arapaho   95
Area defence missiles   9, 85
Aster   108
Automation   100

Base-bleed   20
BLPG   20
BMARC   95
Breda Fast Forty gun   44
Breda Sea Cobra gun   47
British Aerospace   54, 67, 93

Canard control   58
Cardinal Points Procurement   2, 102
Close in weapon system (CIWS)   10, 43
Contraves   27, 49

Data highway   26
Defence in depth   9

Electromagnetic launchers   100
Exocet   62, 107, 108

Fieldhouse, Admiral of the Fleet Sir John   xiv
Future missiles   104

Goalkeeper CIWS   47
Guided projectiles   54
Guns
    BLPG   20
    Breda, Fast Forty   44
    Breda, Sea Cobra   47
    CIWS   10, 43
    Goalkeeper   47
    Guided projectiles   54

Medium calibre naval gun   13
Naval gunfire support   8, 16
Naval guns   31
Oerlikon guns   32
Oto Melara guns   34, 36, 56
RLPG   20
Seaguard   27, 49
Technology, naval gun   18
Vickers 4.5" MK 8. Naval Gun   40

High energy lasers   100

Information technology   26
Intelligence in missiles   103
ISO containers   94

Javelin   84

Kongsberg   57

Lasers, high energy   100
Layered defence   9
Lightweight Sea Dart   89
Lince system   42

Medium calibre naval gun   13
Merchant ships as weapon platforms   93
Missiles
    Agility in   22
    Albatros   80
    ANS   67, 105
    Anti-ship   57
    Area defence   9, 85
    Aster   108
    Canard control of   58
    Exocet   62, 107, 108
    Future   104
    Intelligence in   103
    Javelin   84
    Lightweight Sea Dart   89
    Otomat   3, 73
    Penguin   57

Missiles—*continued*
   Point defence   9, 12, 77
   Seacat   77, 80
   Sea Dart   86
   Sea Eagle   67
   Sea-skimming   1, 30
   Sea Skua   70
   Seastreak   80
   Seawolf   77
   SLAM   76
   Support defence   12, 92
   Technology   22
   Vertical launched   23, 78
MLRS   101
Modularity   27
Multiple channels of fire   11
Munitions   19
Mutual protection   12

Naval gunfire support   8, 16
Naval guns   31
New weapons   100

Oerlikon guns   32
Operational Employment of Weapons   5
Organic air support   8
Otomat   3, 73
Oto Melara   4, 54
Oto Melara Guns   34, 36, 56

Penguin   57
Pickets   12
PIF-PAF   108
Point defence missile system (PDMS)   9, 12, 77
Precision guided munitions   16, 21, 54

Propulsion   20

Reliability   2, 101
RFA Reliant   95
RLPG   20

Saturation attacks   11
SCADS   94
Seacat   77, 80
Sea Dart   86
Sea Eagle   67
Seaguard   27, 49
Sea-skimming missile   1, 30
Sea Skua   70
Seastreak   80
Seawolf   77
Short Brothers   76, 77
Signaal   47
SLAM   76
Smith, Captain John   5
Support defence missile system   12, 92

Technology, missile   22
Technology, naval gun   18
Threat assessment   6
Thrust vector control   22

Vertical launched missiles   23, 78
Vickers 4.5″ MK 8. Naval Gun   40
Vickers Shipbuilding and Engineering Ltd   36, 76

Weapon system architecture   26, 101